Until the Darkness Takes Us

Until The Darkness Takes Us
NATHAN GRAY

DARK GOSPEL TRANSMISSIONS

Copyright © 2016 Nathan Gray

Published by
Dark Gospel Transmissions, LLC
PO box 134
Westerville, OH 43086
www.DarkGospelTransmissions.com

All rights reserved.
ISBN-13: 978-0-692-80755-2

CONTENTS

Acknowlegements 7
Foreword 9
Preface 11

Movement I. (darkness)
  I. Heathen Blood 19
  II. Lusus Naturae 24
  III. Skin 36

Movement II. (chaos)
  IV. Desire 62
  V. Damascus 64
  VII. Set Up 93
  VII. Anthemic Hearts 100

Movement III. (rebirth)
  VIII. At War 110
  IX. Remains 119
  X. Memento Mori 128
  XI. Until The Darkness Takes Us 130
  XII. Jettison 146

The Epilogue
  XIII. Dark Fire 158

Appendix 161

To my fans, my friends, my family, and my enemies...
This book is for me, and for you.
I am forever in your debt for the man
you have helped me to become.

SALUT!

ACKNOWLEDGEMENTS

My deepest gratitude to everyone who lent their time and talents to helping me complete this Masterwork of Catharsis, most especially:

My doppelgänger Matt Paradise, for volunteering to offer fresh eyes to the final editing process. Kevin I. Slaughter for patiently answering a hundred questions about how to produce a book, for formatting the end product, and for providing questionable wit at a moment's notice. Elizabeth Salome for assisting me in crafting my word chaos. Katie Gray, Karin & Barry Gray, Miranda Brewer, Chad Istvan, Jacob Head, Brian Wilson and Sandy Peters Castleberry for fact checking my memories when my brain couldn't seem to remember clearly the how's and when's of my past. The talented lady behind Antikvnst and Mr. Tony Karnes for providing art to compliment the book. Maestro Peter H. Gilmore for offering insight and encouragement in his uniquely distinguished way, and his lovely bride Peggy Nadramia, for her constant support of each of my endeavors.

My bands and the people in them whom I am proud to have created music with along the years—boysetsfire, The New Recruits, The Casting Out, I AM HERESY, and Dan Smith, my partner in Nathan Gray Collective.

My friends and family for being a wonderful support system through all phases of life.

A sincere and joyous thank you to you all for being a constant source of inspiration for this book, and beyond.

wilkes-barre fest
1999 june18/19th

glenn doring
before i break
the kill quota
the ultimate warriors
cross my heart
the judas factor
jersey
tristeza
9lives
notaword
bedford
franklin
world inferno friendship society
fall silent
boy sets fire
grade
combat wounded veteran
reversal of man

FOREWORD

Anyone who has ever interacted with Nathan Gray will tell you that he is special. Whether they loved him or hated him, the power he exudes is undeniable. It is one part admirable and awe-inspiring, and one part unnerving, just as it should be. I have watched people go from vehemently arguing with him, to agreeing with, praising, and befriending him, all in a matter of minutes. I have seen people beg him to lend just a moment of his time to a hurting friend, in an effort to ease their pain. I have watched swarms of people, dripping with sweat in a windowless room or standing shoulder to shoulder in the rain, sway in waves—hundreds, thousands deep—heads thrown back and singing along to his anthems, experiencing an extraordinary moment they will never forget. He has quietly and inconspicuously steadied his nervous hands before taking the podium and spinning an entire room of people in his palm. Crafted a house into a home. Carried the heavy hearted, fought tooth and nail for his family and friends, and inspired so many of us to be better. To be our very best.

Perhaps most importantly though, I have watched him push aside fear and doubt to arrive to this place today. The one where you—friends, family, and fans—hold his messy, painful, sometimes embarrassing, often exciting, often heartbreaking, but fiercely victorious life story in your hands. Aside from being an artist, a writer, a tireless creator and diligent worker, a teacher, a husband, a son, a father, and friend, Nathan Gray is a Human. One who continuously pushes himself further against and into his comfort zones, setting his mind to overcoming his own demons. And to the top, he has risen! I can think of no better example of inspiration than the one his life story offers. Anything he has put his mind to has come to fruition in a firestorm of passion and fervency.

The only thing he fears, is time.

My hope for each of you who reads this autobiography, this manifesto, is that you see Nathan in a new light and are inspired by his ascension into his own kingdom by creating and defining his own success. I'm so glad he's decided to invest into all of you with this book and encourage you to create *your* own futures. Those who stand with him are always shown their own greatness. Take responsibility for your past, and for your tomorrows.

"The death of god is the birth of human potential."

e. s.

PREFACE

The book you are now holding began with a simple idea that flourished into an obsessive need to tell my story. When I began to put down all the pieces that were begging to be written, it came out in a combination of prose, ritual, and frank storytelling—sometimes frantic, sometimes controlled, but always very true to myself.

People have asked me why and when I decided to pen my life story. To put it rather simply, it was just time. I needed the catharsis that would come with facing my fears as they lay within an open book. I needed to bleed out and into the world my vibrant catastrophe, as well as the triumphant success that has come from it, which has, most importantly, come by my own hand and on my own terms.

Compiling all of this was often a painful struggle, but most certainly necessary. Through telling my story, and inspiring others to take in my words, I may gain a certain immortality... or the closest to such that someone like me could ever hope to. It is admittedly a selfish desire, which may garnish altruistic results if it motivates, helps, and heals others with its message. I sincerely hope that through edifying my need to encourage, enkindle, and provoke, that those reading these words will feel exactly that.

This has not been an easy journey, but no goal worth reaching ever starts in such a manner.

I give you... Me.

MOVEMENT I.

I. HEATHEN BLOOD

Bow down / Cry out for a reason to live / For a reason to die
Holy holy god of mercy / In these killing fields your will is done

IN THE BEGINNING THERE WAS A VOID, IN THE BEGINNING THERE WAS FEAR.

"YOU MUST SUFFER FOR CHRIST!" The more I bled for him, the more righteous I was set to become. And so I bled into my boots. I marched and I bled and I suffered for his plan. All the while, being told that I was unworthy, and all that I could offer was my unwavering devotion in hopes that it will be enough.

When probing hands demanded me to kneel and open—kneel and do as I am told behind hushed doors—I consoled my shame with dreams of a promised Heaven, prayers falling fast from my lips, palms high, begging for a reason. My chasteness was savagely spun into a forgotten memory, but surely my suffering was holy, as it was delivered to me over and again by pious men of God himself.

Carnal Stigmata, my cross to bear.
And still, denied my mercy.

Knees bruised from repetition, I carried my victimhood in my belly—comforted by its burning consistency and feeling as though I deserved nothing better. I felt powerless to stop this torment, and so I inspired it instead, taking that bit of control and wielding it as my weapon. What better way to battle for my place with my God, than armed to the teeth? My God wanted this for me. He wanted me to endure this nightmare for him: an ultimate test of his Will.

| | | | |

In a matter of memory, my life begins at Decade One.

My father celebrated my 10th so joyfully that year, it is pasted onto my psyche as the beginning of Me. Housed in love on North Chapel Street within the tiniest of broken down walls, I knew nothing of anguish or of sin, but everything of warmth and devotion and family. My parents—teachers and mentors and keepers of the purest faith—taught me that we were always moving forward, a lesson that I've held dear since. No matter who I've been or where I've been, they have loved me fiercely and sought to provide me everything Heaven & Earth could offer.

I, in turn, wished to be my best for them. Be godly and good. Productive. Spiritual. Successful. Happy. When I was asked by a church elder to let the Holy Spirit speak through me, I sobbed because the words would not come. And so, I faked the tongue; arms reaching, gibberish coming from my lungs. The perception of Spirit moved. Where the church was rough with their love, my parents were all that was good and kind.

Called to the South, we made a pilgrimage shortly after that warm recollection of birthday ten to the land I came to know as my personal Purgatory. Here we lived, suffocatingly immersed in Christ, growing and learning. Compound charm. Services Wednesday and Sunday and back again and everywhere in between; classes on the off days. We worshiped and cohabitated in close proximity to one another.

And to the bible college students.

A Predatorial Precinct: Where "moved with the Holy Spirit" meant abuse was just if forgiveness was asked for. Bonus points for flair.

Here on these 27 acres, a simultaneous conditioning begins. Indoctrination. Transgression.

Depravity surrounded me in that holy place. It stalked me in corners. It dug me out upon fingertips that had been folded in prayer not hours before. Experiences that play back to me now like movies, except someone else is the victim. Impossible to verbalize. Dark. Intense. The chains that bound me as a child of God, locked tight and used against me in the most horrific acts of betrayal. One thousand and ninety five days of dignity, stolen.

In a molotov cocktail of fear, confusion, shame and anxiety about what was happening to me, I found myself in a place where my sole defense mechanism was taking the only control available to me in this twisted infliction. Complacent in my resolve, I arrived at a place where I accepted and allowed myself to continue being a victim, because it was all I knew.

If I thanked God for anything during that time, it was for delivering me my only light in the darkness. A solitary, golden-haired friend, protector and confidant. An angel in his own right. And my parents—my beautiful, wonderful parents, who didn't know.

Couldn't have known.

Beyond The Stigmata, there was so much pressure. Repetitive and heavy. Born with sin, yet striving to live a life without it. Day in and day out terrorized with stories of wickedness; Youth Group produced a catalogue of horror scripts. Every song we recited in unison telling us that we were damaged and unworthy, and must beg God for his mercy. We, children! We were unclean. Impure. Wicked. All Earthly delights a pathway to Hell.

Even the verbiage laid into us...

servant
humble
grovel
blood

Each a calculated weapon to keep us on our knees—compliant and scared. If we were neither of those things, what need would we have for a church at all? In the moment, I took them to be normalities and it wasn't until much later that I recognized them for the emotionally abusive scare tactics that they were. And yet, when my turn came to be blessed in the holy waters, I felt nothing but the innocent joy that came with the game of getting dunked under with my friends. I gave so much of myself, and even more was taken against my will. For what?

When our time on those 27 acres ended, I felt such a great relief. In my naïveté, I assumed that a change in area code would be the catalyst for door shutting. But even as we moved from one end of town to the other and back again, It followed me. It followed me across state lines and over oceans. Sometimes just a cloud in the corner of my mind, often a suffocating fog I couldn't escape from. I was an introvert in those days. Extremely guarded and awkward. Spastic, and unsure.

Nothing like the man I am now.

Everything, Everything, Everything a reminder.

It was no way to live, and I needed to survive. I needed to adapt and overcome.

Beyond ignorance, fear, and shame lies wisdom, power, and self-fulfillment. The personal demons we wrestle with are nothing more than imps of repression—imps we alone can choose to conquer and rise above. There is a natural beast within us all that is tired of being chained up like a common house pet. Triggers are for willful victims and pitiful bystanders. For charlatans that would rather their lives be based on what happened to them, instead of what they can make happen for themselves.

Fuck your triggers. Fuck my triggers.
Keep hitting them until you wear them down, and then rip them off and disarm the gun you've been shooting yourself with.

This is survival. This is vital existence. And in this way, TRUE gods are born.

Save Yourself.

II. LUSUS NATURAE

He's not afraid of the monsters he's afraid of what they hide
There's a wall to keep them in there's a wall to keep you out

THESE GUARDIANS OF THE MIND, AND THESE KEEPERS OF THE HEART.

Stanza One
Even now, I tend to inadvertently spend a lot of time (perhaps too much time) inside my own head. The need to avoid and distract is a matter of urgent self-preservation in these moments. These monuments of struggle -
   To the resting mind,
   To the active mind that requires your full attention—
A deafening silence that there is never proper preparation for.

   All becomes nothing.
   Nothing becomes all.

   Details become subtle nuances,
   And subtle nuances become terrifying.

You become more aware of death and of mortality in these dark silent places. Places that force you to remember, relive, redefine, ready, and reel in Absolute Horror.
   These are the breeding grounds of madness
   The perpetual lunacy of inevitability.
   There is no escape,

   only self defense.

The Charismatic experience is probably vastly different than what most people know of church. There are a handful of musicians that truly encapsulate what my experience with the church was like in those days. Perhaps most memorable for me was Keith Green, an intensely passionate hippie-martyr with a quiverful voice and a humble beauty. He was an evangelist that I, and many others, deeply connected with. If you were part of the Charismatic church in those days, you knew who Keith Green was. His songs of submission were so fervent that even the most lukewarm of believers wanted to be on their knees alongside him. His music was honest and pure, and it was extremely hard not to respect that sort of devotion, despite how one may have felt about the subject matter. As far as spiritual music goes, there really just isn't anything like that in the modern world.

Keith's songs perfectly reflected the teachings of the church, which was a message of love, peace and gentleness, while somehow simultaneously making people feel like garbage. They were a call for action in your unworthy devotion; to live out your mission, bring the word of God to the world, love each other and be living examples of piety. We were taught from day one that we were with fault, and that no one would ever accept all of those faults like Jesus Christ. He would love us no matter what, and for that, we owed him our servitude. You may not be good enough alone, but you are good enough through Him, and there was a sort of confidence and security in that slavery.

I looked up to these Christ-like examples such as Green, or another big musician at the time named Don Francisco, whose "Steeple Song" spoke out against mega-churches. It seems somewhat oxymoronic now to have been looking for leadership in people who were devoted to their own submission, but I did. We all did. We looked up to the slaves, and wanted to be more like them. If we were to envy or strive to be the masters—those who succeed and were doing for themselves—we would be considered to be sinful. Because I was always so deeply moved by the passion Keith Green delivered in his music, I have always strived to bring the same spirit to my own, albeit with a much different subject matter. I will absolutely never forget when he died. The plane he was in went down in 1982, and it rocked so many of us to lose such a powerful force in the ministry. (Looking back at the type of man he was, I would wager that if he knew that plane was going down, he was elated that his day had come, and that he was off to meet his king in Heaven.)

While somewhat difficult to verbalize exactly what the Charismatic church is, I can attempt to explain what might make it different. To start, within the Charismatic church, there is a lot of focus on the spiritual realm, which often manifests in the physical world when someone is filled with the Holy Spirit so intensely, that it can bring about physical reactions. These reactions are often oddities such as speaking in tongues or what we called "falling out in the Spirit" where a person is so consumed with the emotion of what they are experiencing, they may tremble, fall, or even faint. While unusual occurrences to most, these were very normal everyday responses to being filled with the Holy Spirit within my church.

Something I am able to look back on now and recognize as the mass delusion it was is the idea of Spiritual Warfare and living within both the physical and spiritual worlds. We were incessantly told that we were surrounded by both angels and demons at all times, and that we were locked in a never-ending battle against the demons. These spirits were allegedly flying about the unseen world, circling us and watching. Waiting. Even if you couldn't see them in your physical world, they were there. The burden to protect yourself and your family from demons who are hungry for your righteous blood is on you. And it is heavy. So heavy. Every now and then, some church member would report seeing them, sending waves of terror across the community. And how were we to protect ourselves from these evil spirits? Worship. Prayer. Shouting "in the name of Jesus Christ!" whenever necessary. (Satan recoils whenever he even hears the name of Jesus, you know. Seriously. It's like garlic to a vampire and silver bullets to a werewolf.) I lived in constant fear of these demons, terrified that they would take over my body and mind, and that I would be taken from God and my family, doomed to burn in hell for eternity. Just horrible things for a young kid to have on his heart. Now that I have grown past that part of my life, I have taken a particular interest in demonology, finding the symbolism (and the taboo of it) to be fun. Removing the power of fear in that manner has been incredibly therapeutic.

Speaking in tongues, falling out in the spirit, seeing angels and demons cross from the spiritual to physical world, all these sorts of things were referred to as "Gifts of the Holy Spirit," and while I never experienced such phenomena myself, I remember being extremely covetous of those who did, aching to know why God chose to speak with them, and not with me. At the time, it never really occurred to me that while I was lamenting the fact that I wasn't receiving these positive gifts, I was living in fear of punishments that I wasn't receiving either. There's a disconnect between the two that I missed.

Everyone also had a story. A "Testimony." Testimonies were the tale of how one came to Christ. At first, it seemed that everyone's testimony followed the same sort of formula: Wicked sinner, down and out. Probably addicted to drugs or alcohol. Maybe a delinquent of some sort. Definitely burdened with some sort of mental or physical ailment like schizophrenia or homosexuality. There was always some grandiose turning point like a bad acid trip or a near-death experience, during which God spoke to them and they found their way home to Him. After a while though, the shock factor of such stories wore off and the stories became more normal and reactionary, yet far more manipulative and frightening. Suddenly, everyone's testimony was something along the lines of, "I was a good person, but just still not good enough. I never hurt nobody, never let a drop of liquor touch my lips, but I felt a void. Something was still missing in my life. And what was missing was Jesus Christ." It was a bit like watching those commercials asking if you are depressed, listing vague symptoms that literally every person on Earth has felt a few times, when suddenly you find yourself saying to the TV, "Yes I DO sometimes feel sad!" And there you go, off and running to your doctor, desperate to try the newest pharmaceutical that promises to fix what ails you.

I didn't have a Testimony. I was simply born into faith. I definitely felt jealous of people who had these amazing stories of how they came to Christ, just as I envied those who had the Gifts of the Holy Spirit. These people overcame great odds and evils, only to find their triumph. I felt a little left out! I suppose now though, you could consider this book my Testimony in reverse; child broken by abuse and religion, grows up to realize he is his OWN god, makes amazing path for himself. Lives happily ever after.

The Charismatic church does have similarities with other religions. Altar Calls were commonplace, which bear a strong resemblance to the practice of Confession or Penance for Catholics. At the end of every service, church Elders would line the stage, and we were all told to bow our heads while the Pastor asked if anyone needed to come back to or strengthen their relationship with Jesus. If you had some transgressions you needed to get right about, you could come see one of the Elders, who would listen to you and pray with you as you ask for absolution and a renewed faith. I participated in Altar Call several times, often without having a specific reason, but just in case I had done something to upset God that I didn't know about. I became somewhat obsessed with asking for forgiveness even if I had nothing in particular to ask forgiveness from. Compulsive repentance. I was genuinely terrified that there were things I might have unknowingly done to displease him. I had this End Times anxiety that I needed to be sure my soul was ready for, often exacerbated by the doomsday buzz in the congregation when things like credit cards became a thing. (We were told that barcodes were the sign of the Beast, proof positive that the Antichrist was coming.) And while many *acted* terrified of such a fate, the Martyr Syndrome was very real. They couldn't wait to be proven right and to die in the name of Jesus Christ, holding fast to their faith. For me though, it just created this crushing feeling of dread and impending doom that caused me tremendous anxiety.

Learning how to overcome is a sticky, painful process—especially at such a young and confusing age. Three steps forward, two back: ElevenTwelveThirteenFourteen, you were the hardest years of my life. Spinning out, and scared, everything that could go wrong, did. And at that time (admittedly, even now) there was simply no way for me to avoid conversations and situations that would transport me, against my will, back to The Stigmata and that place of fear. Body and mind, not yet working in tandem, I was pleading for salvation, desperate to be relieved of this lewd torment that had become all I knew, and God just didn't seem to be listening. Where was my Savior? Why wasn't He stepping in to rescue me?

I remember very clearly my first experiences with the horror classics. *Frankenstein, Jekyll & Hyde, The Invisible Man, Dracula*—all films I remember watching with my mother at a very young age. I felt an immediate and unspoken kinship with these mysterious, magical men. They were awe-inspiring! They were the beast within personified: evolutionary beauty, power and grace. Most often made savage at the will of others, they were shamed, hurt, preyed upon, vilified, and full of animal instinct they could not control. They were fragile and misunderstood. Passionate, and intense creeps in a world of hateful sheep. I reacted with such heartfelt sadness and empathy at the moving images of them being victimized, just wracked with both a deep anguish for them, and a violent contempt for the herd who sought to harm them. I felt as though only I could see past their snarling teeth and guarded gait to recognize the child locked inside of them. It was deeply therapeutic to identify with their torment, and I quickly learned how to pull them over me like a blanket.

They were me and I was them.

In the name of self-preservation, I have learned that saying "No" to accessing the depths of my most horrifying memories has made me stronger. Much like a physician might induce a coma to heal his patient, invoking these monsters is how I found my safe place to do the same, ensuring that I could function in the face of both The Stigmata, and life in general. The monsters became symbolic archetypes that would guard me from my suffering, from my darkest torments, and together we worked to create barriers around my heart and mind. In the face of "triggers," they stood with me, spoke through me, and strengthened me as I moved through the world. As a team, we maintained my sanity. Their attributes, a shield I wielded in moments of animalistic distrust, and my teachers while I carefully studied and harnessed knowledge of the humans around me. The monsters: my barriers, my Black Flame, and my family. Keepers of my pain. What I learned from them dictated how I would react to people and situations for the rest of my life; whether that meant keeping others at bay, or tucking deep the secret of my affliction.

Quite often, both.

Dr. Jekyll & Mr. Hyde, who possessed the awesome power of duality. Jekyll, a fairly "normal" man by day, could transform himself in order to indulge his darker side. Somewhat ironically, being unable to exercise his desires safely, (thanks largely to the herd making him feel wicked) his Hyde side became compulsive.

King Kong, the quintessential, misunderstood gentle giant. Captured and forced to have his carnality stripped from him, he met his fate at the bottom of a skyscraper after he had moved to protect a woman in distress.

Dr. *Frankenstein* was a creator. A brilliant man who sought to defy the laws of God and man, by working to manifest artificial life.

The Hunchback of Notre Dame, Victor Hugo's novel which later became my most cherished of all Disney films, depicts the tale of an "imperfect" human abused by those called to do so by a higher power.

And *The Wolf Man,* one of my favorite horror classics. He, the plagued animal who was afflicted by his inability to restrain his fervor.

Comic books were another source of empathetic championing for me. Even when I was very young, before The Stigmata stormed into my life, I felt most drawn to the more human characters like Batman, Daredevil, Sgt. Rock, or the Punisher—normal people who forged through extraordinary pain and created themselves anew. They were the dark, self-made heroes. Complex and fueled by their afflictions, they all became vigilantes. I carried these heroes with me, and developed a deeper understanding of them as my own tragedies began to line up with theirs.

As I aged, I felt a shifting in my connection to these monsters and heroes—one from general empathy, to the immensely liberating feeling that came with embracing what I could now see as the positive aspects of both the monster *and* their creator. Vampire and Host. Master and slave.

Which brought me here, to the mighty *Dracula*, who became my Pinnacle. The ultimate Is To Be.

Dracula's "monster" was less about shame and more about embracing the darkness within. He was the embodiment of class, sensuality and strength, and he possessed the powers of influence that could lay the world at his feet. Even those who abhorred him, could not help but be drawn in by his magic and charm. He showed us that the affection between master and slave—monster and creator—is full of all-consuming passion, and its soul sharing intimacy is vastly deeper and wildly more intense than an ordinary love. A vampiric relationship is the absolute epitome of commitment, and truly transcends all mortal relationships.

> *"I ask for so little. Just let me rule you, and you can have everything that you want... Just fear me, love me, and do as I say, and I will be your slave"*

When I look at the connection between vampire and his mortal life-source, I see a mutually beneficial union; one in which the vampire, like a bee with a flower, takes what he needs and then provides in kind exactly what his victim desires. It is entirely symbiotic in nature, master and slave depending on each other for survival. A give and take situation. It is primal, ethereal, and unrivaled; an incredibly powerful connection that is most certainly esoteric in nature. Because Vampire and Host are eternally bound together, each party effortlessly, but earnestly, takes on special roles in the relationship—each as powerful as the other, and like the sadist and the masochist, neither partner is weak; they simply fit together.

Perhaps the most poetic element of the Vampire, is that his power is two-fold. He certainly has the strength to take everything he needs, emptying his Host carelessly and completely (as he would with a dreadfully average human) but he chooses instead to inject his life force back into his Host, thereby making her immortally his.

It begins with a deliberate hunt. Rather than wasting (or worse, draining!) his own energy filling himself with subpar lifeblood, the Vampire will use his intuition to read those around him, choosing only the most ideal Host. Once in his grasp, his initial handling of the Host often invokes both fear and respect, which are wholly appropriate responses to his power. There is often a bit of a trial period, during which the Vampire tests his Host to ensure her worthiness to him. However, the Vampire is not malicious in his intent. Once he is certain that she will provide the purest, most powerful of energy, he does not manipulate his Host because there is no need to. He loves her, and she is already enthusiastically his, and to do so would break that trust. She submits to his will gleefully, graciously, and moves to expend all her energy into his happiness and success. In turn, the Vampire accepts full responsibility for his Host as his property. He encourages her continued growth, (for he thrives on only the highest quality lifeblood) and puts forth great effort into the constant reading of and attending to her physical and emotional needs. This unabated pouring out into and inspiring of each other, creates a dependency that is extremely productive and loving, and that back and forth is what creates immortality in both the relationship, and the individuals themselves.

The immortality the Vampire offers is metaphorical. The true vampire holds an estimable position in life, and once his Host expounds her energy into him, her efforts are, too, remembered. Even the Holy Bible shows us evidence of this. Consider Mary Magdalene's dedication to Jesus. Always extraordinarily devoted, she even anoints him with the most expensive perfume before his crucifixion. She is mocked, the people aghast, but she is unmoved by their taunting, and Jesus defends her saying, *"She has done a beautiful thing to me... When she poured this perfume on my body, she did it to prepare me for burial. Truly I tell you, wherever this gospel is preached throughout the world, what she has done will also be told, in memory of her."* Matthew 26:6-13

As much as a Vampire seeks and chooses his Host, she too, carefully accepts her mate. The gift of self is not to be given arbitrarily, and so she is incredibly discriminate in who she submits to. An ideal Host will passionately and eagerly gift her entire self to her Vampire, devoting all energy to his happiness and success. Every spark she possesses will become flames within the torch of the Vampire, and she is always willing to gift for the greater good. The Host would feel lucky to belong to her Vampire, but also know that she TOO is powerful, and that her Vampire deserves her—the very best. (After all, there is a reason the Vampire has sought her out, and captured her as his own.) Even so, she must tirelessly work to provide sustainable, inspiring, encouraging, devoted, and positive lifeblood each and every day. Her devotion and the gifting of herself to the Vampire is what gives her pleasure. Its all-encompassing nature takes great strength and self-awareness, but the reward is sweet. It is a conscious choice she makes to give an incomparable gift that satisfies a primal need... for both of them. When a Host chooses to offer herself completely to another—mentally, physically, emotionally, creatively—it is given out of pure love and pure adoration. It is given rarely and with utmost respect. The Host desires to give her most precious energy to only the most estimable. To one who would know both how to honor her gift, and how to cherish her in return.

Together, Vampire and Host nurture a rare and intense partnership that benefits, fulfills, and heals in a way that nothing else can.

These self-made heroes, carnal monsters and their fantastic creators will always be necessary extensions of our fragile, mortal psyches. As a child, I (and no doubt, many of you) was told over and over again that my inherent nature was evil, sinful, and dirty. Not only did these characters allow me to begin attempting to make peace with my true nature, they showed me how to tend to the wounds inflicted upon me, and ensure that they would never revisit. If we are to be our own gods, we must learn to heal ourselves. Personal growth and a move forward requires extremely honest introspection, a lesson I had just then begun to wrap my head around, my knees weak from the crushing weight of indoctrinated shame.

III. SKIN

My mind keeps telling me stop before I go too far
But my heart's racing to taste the depth of who we are

LIKE HONEY COATED APPLE SEEDS,
THIS BLESSED SIN IS SWEET
    Fire will surely burn.
    Yet tauntingly it dances, seductive and brilliant,
    daring us to drag our fingers across its tongue.
    Batted eyes and thrashing beats. The curve of a hip.
    A devil's kiss, I pray.
    Feed and Feed and Feed and Repent.
    Tithe, Binge & Purge: cyclic loathing.

When we are children, we take anything an adult tells us at face value, no matter how ridiculous it may seem in hindsight—that is the danger of indoctrination. Young minds, ready for shaping, eager to please. Yet no matter what narrative is laid into us, the natural, carnal desire for what brings pleasure is always there, waiting for satiation. And so begins the battle within: the struggle of resolving what we know as inherent truths, against the alleged truths from the lips of Jesus Christ.

    While on the 27, we were subjected to a lot of propaganda surrounding the Satanic Panic and New Age Movement. I remember being shown films about the evils of John Denver, rock music, and even Yoga. Anything that wasn't centered on God was either Satan or a tool that would open the mind to Satan. Interestingly enough, through those very films is where I began to recognize my true nature, although I was too terrified to explore it at the time. One of the films we were shown in Youth Group documented the "secret rituals" of this sort of outlandish and grandiose looking man wearing devil horns. This man was named Anton LaVey, and I was utterly fascinated. Even at that age, I felt as though this man—this anomaly—was full of winking suggestion, and that perhaps much of what he was doing and saying was meant to provoke or play games with the general public. To me, that was awe-inspiring, self assured, and a mark of power. I knew that something so calculated and deliberate surely had to be more than "devil worship" as it was being reduced to.

All the irrefutable tenets force fed to me when I was young were not just simple lies, they were quite literally an abuse of my self-worth. They worked to systematically construct me into a good little soldier for Christ under the guise of making me a "better" person. And perhaps even more terrifying for me as a child was the notion that God was "always watching" to ensure my servitude was up to par. (Naturally, it was said that He was also watching out FOR me. Strangely, I never felt that loving comfort and protection while I was being pushed into hushed corners and desecrated. Funny how that works.) Consequently, not only did I feel stalked and fearful that each move I made might be wrong and I would be struck down for my sins, I also felt a sense of anxiety when my hands were idle. Should I be praying right now instead of hanging out with my friends? Have I given God his due praise today? Has my worshiping been humble and fervent enough?

I was trying so hard to be good in the eyes of God, despite the internal battle I was fighting. I wanted to question, I wanted to test the waters, I wanted to explore the glaring dichotomies I was experiencing, but I was genuinely terrified of the horrifying repercussions said to be waiting for me, and so I did a lot of self-repressing. A lot. Any time I allowed myself to give in to my curiosities or desires in ANY way, I would feel as though I had failed. I know now that those perceived failures were actually steps forward towards embracing myself, but at the time, it was a heavy burden to carry. Stone by stone, cast straight into my lungs.

My self-imposed penitence was flogging myself with prayer, begging to be forgiven.

And what were the two most critical needs to fill at that time? Music and Sex... what else does a teenage boy care about? I have this memory, living on the 27, devouring the beautiful rhythms on a cassette tape I had been keeping hidden away in my room. I felt intensely connected to the beats as they wound up into the tape, but after a few feedings upon its intoxicating magic, I burned the cassette. I was terrified that actual demons would come into my room and poke my ears until they bled at night, a fate we were warned of in Youth Group meetings. Satan was in rock music, you know, and within those sinful notes is how he would stray us from our holy paths.

The joy of Compound Charm was that everything we "needed" was made available to us on that campus. Even what was provided to us for reading or listening to was controlled. There was a tiny store on campus that offered a selection of books and music, as well as a small library. In the library were audio tapes that served much like those panic inducing films we were shown. The tapes were frantically narrated by a preacher, detailing the dangers of rock music and desperate to save you from the clutches of Satan's symphonies. He would launch into lengthy descriptions of how the Devil was controlling children through backmasking, hidden meanings within the lyrics, and how the songs were doling out diabolical instructions that would compel anyone who listened to commit all sorts of horrors. The tapes would play tiny bits and pieces of popular songs before the narrator would interrupt to explain what evils we had just heard, giving you just enough of the actual song to get the gist, but not enough to have to fear the loss of your soul over hearing, "In this song by the Dead Kennedys, from the disturbing album *Fresh Fruit for Rotting Vegetables,* these punk rock demons are telling the listener to kill children." Everything they were saying was so wildly off base. They even claimed that KISS was a punk band. But I checked those tapes out often because that was my only way to hear new music at the time. Each song blew hot wind on the fire in my chest. I had to hear more—I needed it like air, but I had no idea how to get more of it.

We were totally immersed in our faith back then. We went to church twice a week for worship and attended Youth Group meetings, workshops, holiday meet-ups and evangelized to the community in between. Even my first few concerts were Christ-centered. (Although I am told that my VERY first concert was Bob Dylan, when my mother was still pregnant with me.) This all-consuming culture seemed natural at the time, and that was how we socialized since all of our friends (and generally *only* our friends) were at each function. Because of this, there was little opportunity to be challenged in our resolve, which was actually just fine by me. Back then, I was much more introverted and hated confrontation—and yes, I am aware how that may seem impossible to those who know me now—and I honestly wouldn't have had any idea how to respond to a challenge of my faith. Embarrassingly, I was committed to it, but likely could not have told you WHY.

I remember one very specific time I was out evangelizing with my youth group. We were passing out tracts on the street when we ran into some punk kids at the park, and I remember immediately feeling so stupid and so humiliated, my cheeks lighting up instantly. I flat out refused to go talk to them with my friends, hiding across the lawn instead. One of them actually came over to me and asked if I was with the others in my group and I immediately denied it, a knee-jerk reaction that I felt intensely guilty for later. But I thought these kids were so badass. I had been secretly and cautiously experimenting with punk, hardcore, and rock music through those library tapes, and these kids embodied the forbidden fruit that I longed for. I watched my friends and our youth group leader attempt to win the punks over, my leader making mortifying attempts to use hip, young buzzwords to draw them in. The punk kids saw right through all of us, though. It was really the first time anyone had ever called me on my faith like that. They were confident and bold in their beliefs (or lack thereof) and I envied that. They weren't hostile, which in all honesty we likely would've loved—being met with anger would've only solidified our martyrdom as we bore witness to Satan speaking through these poor souls. When one of the punks grew tired of having his space invaded by people unwilling to hear what HE had to say in response to them, he simply walked over to his car and put on "Peace Sells" by Megadeth, cranked up the volume, and just stood there. It was the coolest fucking thing I'd ever seen. In that moment I realized how much better it was to be a master and leader in that manner than to do so on bended knee. Even more impressive to me was that these kids were doing and saying what they were, challenging us and Jesus Christ himself, and not ONE of them had been struck by lightning for doing so.

    To exacerbate my uncertainty, I constantly found myself living out experiences that left me wondering if my fears were perhaps not so far-fetched. Once, some friends and I skipped church, and as we drove around listening to Iron Maiden's "The Number of the Beast," the kid driving the car I was in broadsided another vehicle. We all got hurt. I even broke the cartilage in my nose. In my head, I knew that we were being punished for skipping church. God was upset with us, and that's why our car was in an accident. Ridiculous, but at the time, it was enough to scare me straight again for a while.

Always, backsliding.

Binge & Purge: cyclic loathing.

There is an exciting, lustful, carnal beast within us all. It is the beautiful spark that drives us forward, yet one of the first "sins" we are taught to control is that very nature. Pleasures of the flesh deemed the pathway to death—the act of sex, sullied with shame and dishonor, clinically stripped of its delights. We are taught that the primality of lust is to be used within the confines of marriage only, squelching our natural instinct to find pleasure, warmth, and orgasmic joy through ways not deemed "of God's will" by the church. We are taught that lust is the Devil that creates disease, depression, and overpopulation. It is cultic control: nothing more, and nothing less. Mental, emotional, and physical slavery enforced through guilt, shame, self-loathing, and confusion. As I got older, thanks in part to that horrible conditioning, sex FELT shameful, wrong and dirty to me. Participating in it felt like an insincere act, and was stripped of enjoyment—a mindset towards sexuality I stand here and admit took a very long time to shake off. Definitely longer than it should have. For many of my adult years, I only sought out emotionally unfulfilling casual sexual encounters or borderline abusive relationships. If I didn't have love and meaning in sex, it didn't have to hurt.

Despite all of that, I was still curious, and I of course felt the pull of that natural need. When I was a young teen, my friends and I would sneak into nearby abandoned houses where older kids would hide out to drink, smoke, and engage in all the debauchery a high-schooler could get themselves into. I would often find adult magazines and peek through them, cheeks aflame with embarrassment, fear, and a wild, lusty desire. Sometimes I would roll them up and tuck them into my clothes, slipping undetected into my room later, and hiding them in my closet. My dad would almost always find them, scolding me for my indiscretion.

Always, backsliding.

Binge & Purge: cyclic loathing.

The movement itself was gross but genuinely didn't feel hateful, although it truly was hate wrapped in love and ignorance. We felt sorry for people with such maladies as homosexuality because they had to carry that bondage with them straight to hell. We felt that it was our purpose to help save these people from themselves. "Hate the sin, love the sinner!" A disgusting, backhanded thing to say, but that is how we were taught to approach such things, despite the fact that the two cannot be separated. Or even that the application of the term "sin" itself is entirely relative. I am horrified to say that I participated in this vile display once when I wrote an article about homosexuality that was published in a Youth Group zine. Regurgitating what I had been spoon-fed, I spoke of how homosexuals did not understand that they were sinners and needed to be told so, with love. I hate looking back to that and I can't help but wonder how many people I hurt with my words. How many people going through some tough times of self-discovery did I make feel like a lesser human? And I should have known better. For all the carnal suffering I was enduring myself, I should have known better than to inflict pain on someone else. But I thought I was doing God's work and service. Tricky.

I assumed that my prayers were finally being answered when a change in leadership brought about wild attitudes on the 27, after which my parents (and a great deal of others) packed up and moved us out of those godforsaken walls. I was 14 and inside out, but as soon as we made it out of there, I felt the weight begin to lift. The initial rush that came felt like freedom, but it truly wasn't. Not yet. Not for many, many years.

Our next church experience was so much more joyful and lighthearted. 10 tiny pews, and a jovial pastor who made it almost fun again. The message was still stifling, of course, but it didn't feel quite as frightening. Internally, I still struggled with the shame of my carnality, but I began to fear the wild repercussions of life's simple pleasures less and less.

Better still, I was no longer within reach, and at the whim of those probing hands.

I grew up immersed in music, getting my love of folk and Broadway musicals from my parents. As a kid, I was an avid fan of Michael Jackson until the first time I heard Prince, who I became immediately obsessed with. The way he moved and sang was in a league of its own: Poetry in lips and hips. But it really wasn't until I found and accepted rock music that my passion for song ignited. Not long after we left the 27, we were visiting family in the area when a very important turning point in my life occurred. On that pivotal visit, my young family members, fans of punk, gave me some albums to take home. It was not at all the first time I had heard such music (I once had a Cult album confiscated that an older kid at school gave me) but most certainly the first time I had done so without quite so much shame. I took them home and hid them in my room, still a little unsure of the repercussions I might face, but unable to resist pulling them out one by one to feed upon them—The Ramones, The Replacements, Suicidal Tendencies, Nine Inch Nails, Husker Du, Born Against, Minor Threat, Code of Honor, the soundtrack for *Decline Of The Western Civilization*, and the two most defining bands that shaped my love for song at that time; Black Flag and Fear.

I found myself drawn to these very strong, ultra-charismatic frontmen. Bowie. Ving. Rollins. Roth. They became my new monsters, every one of them the Dracula, full of magic and power. I wanted to be them—the Four Horsemen of my apocalypse and rebirth.

Lee Ving of Fear took the stage with a fierce confidence I couldn't dare dream for at that time. He would very intentionally and purposefully taunt his audience. He fed on them, and he knew exactly what he was doing and how to bring out and harness that fire. My first time seeing *The Decline Of Western Civilization,* was completely fucking mind-blowing—it was all about Ving. I had rented the VHS from a place down the street and I was blind to anything else happening on that screen through possibly the first 20 viewings. When I was a kid, my grandparents were some of the only people I knew who had cable. The box had 20 brown push-buttons, and I would slide into the room with the television and punch in the number for MTV and devour the videos on the screen. The first time I saw the video for "Space Oddity," I lost my goddamned mind. David Bowie was otherworldly, androgynous, and full of sex and charisma. The way he moved, his voice, it was completely entrancing. I was driven wild and had to consume everything I could about this man. David Lee Roth, whose "And The Cradle Will Rock" I had first heard through those library tapes, was a walking middle finger to the entire world. When I finally saw the video, that was the end of it for me. I stood there stunned, just enthralled by this man. He was brazen, confident and his bravado was a brand of its own.

The first Black Flag song with Rollins I ever heard was "Drinking and Driving." It was on a tape my friend made for me and when Greg Ginn's guitar part kicked in, it destroyed me. It wasn't so much of a guitar solo as it was just this catchy sort of repetitive noodling. I was hooked, and Black Flag ended up being the very first punk show I ever attended. It was their last tour and they were playing at The Handlebar in Pensacola, so I snuck out of the house to go check out the show. I couldn't have been more than 13 or 14 years old, but it was an experience I will never, ever forget. Rollins commanded the stage as this defiant, dark god. He was a brooding ball of energy that I could not look away from. It scared the shit out of me. The whole experience was just so intense—I was still wildly introverted at the time, and it was just too fucking much. After a few songs, I faded back out the door and went home. Despite how terrified I had been, I was still incredibly intrigued. The memory of it replayed over and over in my head, and I would sit and visualize how he had moved and looked. What he had said. I wanted to be him. No hesitation. That was who I wanted to be. (That show made me so anxious, I didn't even attempt to see another until years later when Screeching Weasel played a skate contest in my hometown. Vastly different experience.)

While you could likely never put these Four Horsemen in the same room without some sort of catastrophe, for me, they all shared a common trait: All four of these men were expressing their carnality without shame. I was not. Not even close. I desperately wanted to be though, and so I began sort of emulating that confidence to the outside world. Mannerisms, nuances. Whatever it took. I would wear their traits like I had with the Monsters, and they would shape how I moved about the world. When chatting with old friends about my past for this book, I was a little shocked that nearly all of them viewed me as a rebellious, confident kid who was unafraid to question authority figures. I didn't feel like that at all, but I was invoking a sort of "fake it 'til you make it" philosophy, which in the end paid off. In retrospect, I think a lot of that rebellion was based in the fact that I didn't fear worldly authority; it was God that I feared.

I absolutely hated school growing up. By the time I graduated, I had attended eight different schools, and virtually every single experience I had was awful. Some of them were public, others were Christian, the tuition for which was always funded by my grandparents. The very first school I actually attended in Florida was a frighteningly strict Christian institution. I came home crying every single day, and my parents pulled me out almost immediately, sending me then to the Christian school associated with the 27. I was always so spastic and misdirected in class, struggling hard with what had happened (or was happening) to me—broken, and acting out in every possible way as I battled through my anger and hurt. I got terrible grades all the way through, though not for lack of intelligence. One of my teachers at Bellview Middle School, an absolutely horrible woman who would often laugh at me and call me stupid in front of the class, had even attempted to transfer me out to a program for students with learning disabilities. After just a few days, my new teacher determined I did not belong there at all and sent me right back. Despite struggling with math a bit, I was more than capable of performing at an acceptable level but I just never cared to sit down, shut up, and apply myself. I never turned in assignments. Never cared to participate. No one was going to tame me. I was too busy being a hyper little asshole, concerned more with making people laugh and getting attention, which for me was an affirmation of my worth. I did a lot of summer school and spent a lot of time in detention. A lot. I was even suspended from school a few times and my father always insisted that I spent the time away from class at work with him, telling me that suspension was "not a vacation." I vividly remember cleaning shelves of random truck parts and assisting the mechanics however they needed it. They all definitely tried their best to make the experience as miserable as possible for me, in hopes that it would "scare me straight."

Several of the schools I attended were very diverse and had a bit of a race/class war within them, but I always made it through by being a class clown, doing completely off the wall shit so people would either leave me alone thinking I was insane, or gravitate towards me, seeing that I was just a goofy and loving kid underneath. It was all a part of my self-priming—a quest to figure out how I could keep protecting and validating myself while I worked through finding who I was and where I was going.

Because we moved around so much within the city, my high school experience was divided up between three different schools, each one vastly different from the others. Freshman year began as awkward as I was, me showing up in horribly preppy clothes, pressed and new. If my memory serves me right, I believe that year they were Garanimals brand from the "elephant collection." Super chic. My parents always insisted that I begin a new school year by making a good impression. They taught me that no matter what, we should always dress and act above where we were at in life. As with most any lesson a parent teaches their child, it wasn't one I appreciated until much later. We didn't have a ton of money growing up, but it never mattered to me. For the most part, we moved in and out of blue collar communities, so I never felt like an outcast in that respect. And while I ate a lot of tomato or peanut butter sandwiches, I knew that my parents loved me, and I loved them. I never felt like I was "without," though I'm sure at some points, we must've been. As soon as I could shed that clumsy entrance to high school life, I latched on to the punk kids in school. Although I never sported bondage pants and mohawks like several of my friends back then, (I eventually did began to dress differently once I started figuring out who I was) I certainly shared a common world view and, most importantly, a love for punk rock. We usually hung out by the trophy case before school began, my friends and I swapping cassette tapes back and forth and looking just apathetic enough to make a point. We got to experience so many new bands in that constant trade off, and I always enjoyed the enthusiastic reviews of what bands we had discovered. The beginning of high school was also my first real foray into having girlfriends. I was so fucking bad at it. I'm weirded out just thinking back on it now… everything was so awkward and I was so uncomfortable in my own skin. Sex was this strange act that I neither knew how to do, or knew how to allow myself to take part in without feeling dirty and ashamed. Always this cycle of wanting very natural things but having said things sullied in some way or another.

Something in me really clicked on during this time of my life, and my path was absolutely realized. I was completely consumed and I knew that there was no way I *wasn't* going to be on stage someday. Interestingly enough, a Prophet who once visited our church told me that one day I would be in a band and travel the world. She told me I was going to have to decide whether or not I would be playing music for God or the Devil. For the longest time, that blew my mind, until it occurred to me that my parents, who were friends of hers, had most likely told her in passing that I was interested in music. As much as music brought me into my faith, it even more so brought me out if it. Back and forth I would go between wanting to submerge into that devil music, and feeling shameful for even entertaining the idea. Eventually, I came to realize that music made me feel much more deeply, helped me cope better, and filled me with a greater sense of purpose than religion ever did. Not overnight, but I did start to make strides, slow and steady over many, many years. The Fear lived in the back of my mind, but I began to listen to it less and less. The Pull was simply too intense to ignore any longer, and I began embracing that Vampiric archetype more and more, humanizing him through how I carried myself. A group of friends who I would often get together and skateboard with started to write some songs here and there, and eventually I decided to try out. The hilarious part is that in the beginning, I was going to play drums and my friend Chad was going to sing. We tried out for the band to Danzig's "Mother." Chad sang about as well as I could play drums and when he left the band, I took over vocals and I nailed it. The band was called Second Nature, and I don't even know if I can verbalize how huge that was for me. It was a gigantic move forward therapeutically and would set me onto my life's work and passion.

I remember my first time on stage very well. We played at a small club called the Nite Owl in Pensacola, and while I was admittedly pretty nervous before the show, everything faded away the moment I stepped on stage. It was like a switch flipped on and my entire world lined right into place. It was the most perfect marriage of everything that I needed so badly in that time, and it all crashed together into a place where I could wear my own carnality proudly. Everything outside of that space suspended, and all I felt was my own strength on that stage. It felt completely natural for me to be up there, and I knew that I was exactly where I was supposed to be. I think what sticks out the most about that show is my dad coming up to me afterwards and saying how impressed he was and that he "did not expect that!" out of me. In talking to old friends, it would seem that most everyone shared that sentiment. Who I was offstage, and who I transformed into on it were night and day. I became that Is To Be.

    I really had only seen a handful of shows before being in my first band. Probably less than a handful, to be honest. I was still very much in my own head and hung out at home alone more often than not. Once Second Nature started playing, I was able to venture out and see more. We opened for a lot of bands back then, almost always at the Nite Owl. EconoChrist had us on their bill once, which was amazing. We saw Green Day play to just a handful of kids, while they were still screening t-shirts out of their van before shows. Bad Brains and Fugazi made stops there, as did many others, and every show was like being reborn as I took in the energy from the room. I enjoyed having things to do and create that gave me a chance to feel strong. It was temporary relief from my own mind, which did not do well when left to its own devices.

    The next high school I attended was in a much more affluent district, and I ended up finding my crew quickly. I was a junior by then, and my parents had (thankfully) given up forcing me to show up in my nice-guy clothes on the first day. I ended up befriending a small group of more new-wave type kids (the more typical punks at this school just seemed to be dicks) and I found myself in a crowd of R.E.M. and Bauhaus fans who always seemed to like me, perhaps because I wasn't a musical purist, finding passion within all types of song. I had been in choir for a couple of years at this point, though the director at the previous school sort of hated me, and with the attitude I carried in those days, it was well deserved. She respected my voice but hated my "I'm punk, fuck the world!" attitude. I'm fairly certain she thought I was a loser. At Pine Forest High School though, I met a sweet woman who would help shape my future. Mrs. Gibson, my choir director, was one of the very few teachers that I remember fondly. I know I was a handful but she saw through my bullshit and liked me anyway, and I desperately needed someone like that in my life. I loved choir. I LOVED singing. But I had such a chip on my shoulder and she just handled me in a sort of "OK, Nathan, shut up and sing" manner, and I always did. She was the very first person in school who saw potential in me. She truly believed I could do something with myself and have a future to be proud of, and it encouraged me to go out and try things. Her presence in my life was monumental. I got to be in her All-State choir group, attend competitions, and perform in shows thanks to her, and a lot of what I've done musically in life has been with her in mind. I still use her teachings and encouragement to push myself to try new things, and I think I owe a big part of me getting to where I am in my life as a musician to her.

Second Nature, while huge in my personal development, didn't get to play together more than a couple of years. Towards the end of my junior year of high school, my parents and I made the move back north to Maryland. To my safety zone. Moving during that time of high school was somewhat of a benefit for me because it allowed me to enter a new school and be whoever I wanted. None of these people knew me as the awkward introvert of my past, and so I pushed down the darkness once again and kicked through the doors as the quintessential punk rock kid. And it worked. I gained popularity and a little bit of confidence, all in one. Admittedly, I was a bit of a loudmouth who liked to show off, always looking for (and finding) my share of trouble, and subsequently, I learned some lessons in taking hits. Less of a loner this time around, I was still a terribly wild entity that, again, found his way into in-school suspension on several occasions. This new school was also where I met a goofy kid wearing black Chucks, peg-rolled jeans, a black trench coat and wore his long hair in a ponytail halfway down his back. He reminded me of the rebel punk in *The Breakfast Club*. That kid's name was Chad Istvan. Chad and I became fast friends, finding that we had a lot in common when it came to music. Being in such a geographically small area, the metalheads, the hippies, and the punks all hung out together because we were all the outcasts. There wasn't such a division between groups like in my previous schools. He and I would get together and play, covering songs by Queensrÿche and Jane's Addiction, just having fun and blowing off steam.

At that high school in North East Maryland, I met Mrs. Porter-Savoy, an English teacher who was another incredibly strong presence in my life back then. She was so hard on me but I knew it was simply because she believed in me. She pushed me to just try to apply myself and when an assignment allowed for free, creative writing, I would empty myself of words and she always seemed visibly proud of my work. But any time she asked me to be critical and structured, my attitude came out and we would butt heads. I didn't want to follow formats and write outlines, I just wanted to write whatever was inside me.

Writing is something I think I've just always done. Even when I was very young, pieces would come together in my head out of nowhere and I had to rush to get them on paper and give them life. At first, the words would manifest as short little stories, but as I grew, they tumbled out as songs and politically fueled essays. I published several collections of my writings in zines as a teenager, and honestly, writing is the one thing I've always felt confident in. (I have no doubt that is exactly what frustrated poor Mrs. Porter-Savy. I could do it. I had it all in me, I was just too stubborn to do it as I was told.) I always wanted to write and share my compositions with others because it offered a certain release that I couldn't get anywhere else. It felt good to create something I was proud of that others responded well to. Lyric writing is very much a free-form outpouring of poetry for me and begins in a stream of consciousness movement from head to fingertips without much direction. When the mood or inspiration strikes, it just comes and doesn't stop until it stops. When it does, I look at how what I've written works within the music and adjust the wording if need be. As a whole, though, the process is (and always has been) rather effortless for me.

Everything in those years was a quest to grow into myself.

Sometime during my senior year of high school, Chad and I began writing songs and formed a legit band called Jones Chapel. A band of nearly indescribable style, we somehow meshed my Shudder To Think to his Voivod. Chad, always a very technical musician, played in these crazy time signatures, and I was looking to push myself lyrically and vocally. We would experiment with political, social, and personal issues that spoke to us, all to the tune of some very purposefully "out there" music. We even played a few local shows and inexplicably found it necessary to cover Jimi Hendrix's "Purple Haze." For some reason, the Newark punks seemed to dig it... still have not figured out that anomaly yet. But it was great experimenting with music in a way I may never had, if it were not for Chad.

During this time, politics became a big deal to me, as I immersed myself into the bravado of Abbie Hoffman, Mikhail Bakunin and Nietzsche. I became somewhat addicted to the chemical release that came with knowing I was right in the midst of verbal discourse, but I still needed reassurance from others—I was terrified of people not accepting me. Somehow, I thought I would save myself if I saved the world. I needed to constantly be at battle with something to keep my mind occupied and away from the dark that scratched at the corners, trying to get to the surface. I believed myself a revolutionary. An angry young man ready to take on "the system." (Little did I realize, "the system" is a bit more complicated and nuanced than I gave it credit for.) I needed to lash out, and what better target than an amorphous, idealized bugbear? Politics became an outlet and whipping boy for a pain and suffering that I could neither speak aloud, nor allow myself to remember.

I was very, very good at covering things, but the more time passed, the harder it became to mask, and everything was about to come to a head.

Like Dr. Jekyll, my own Hyde came out, uninvited, in my sleep.

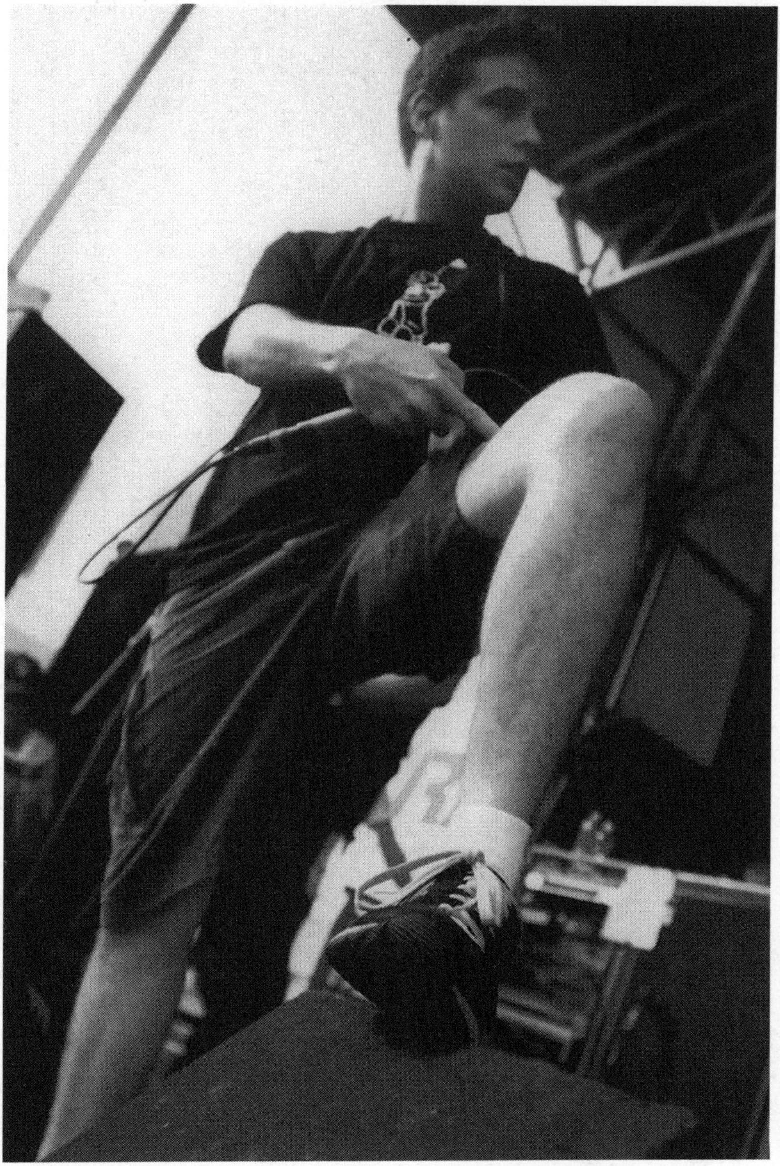

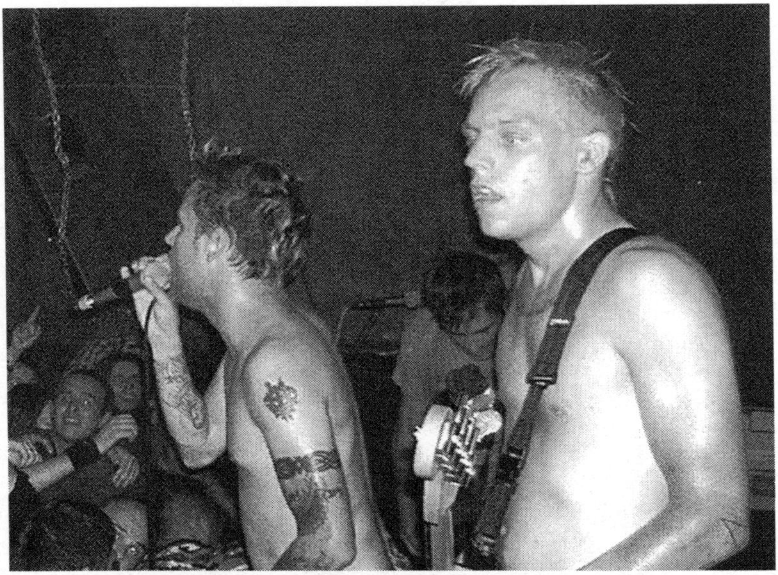

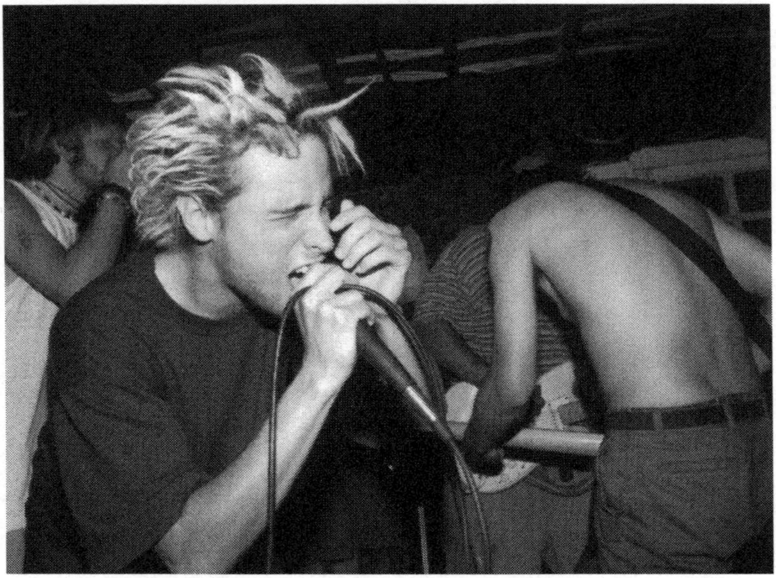

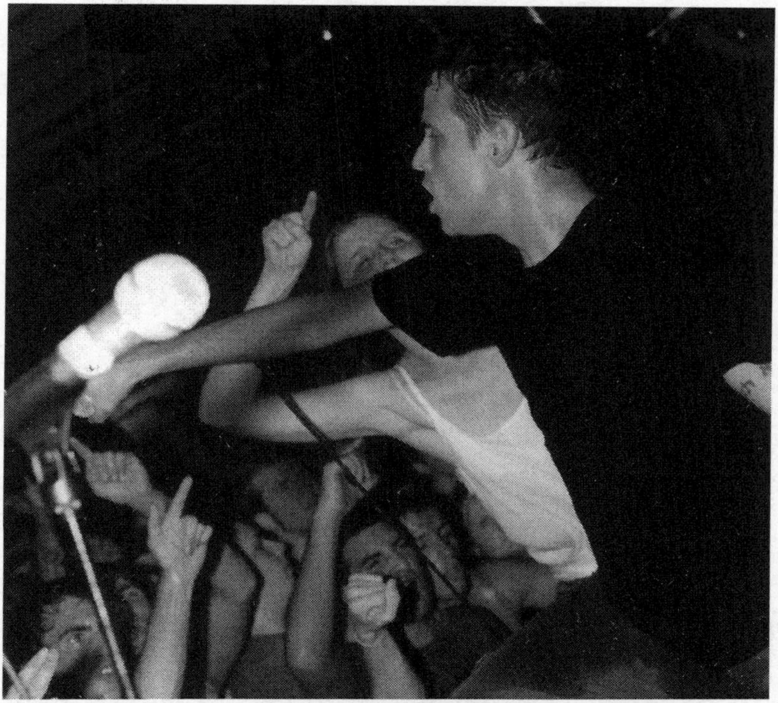

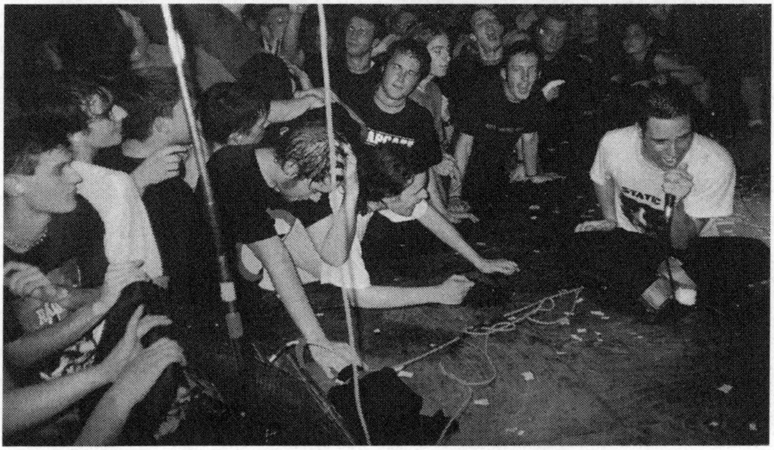

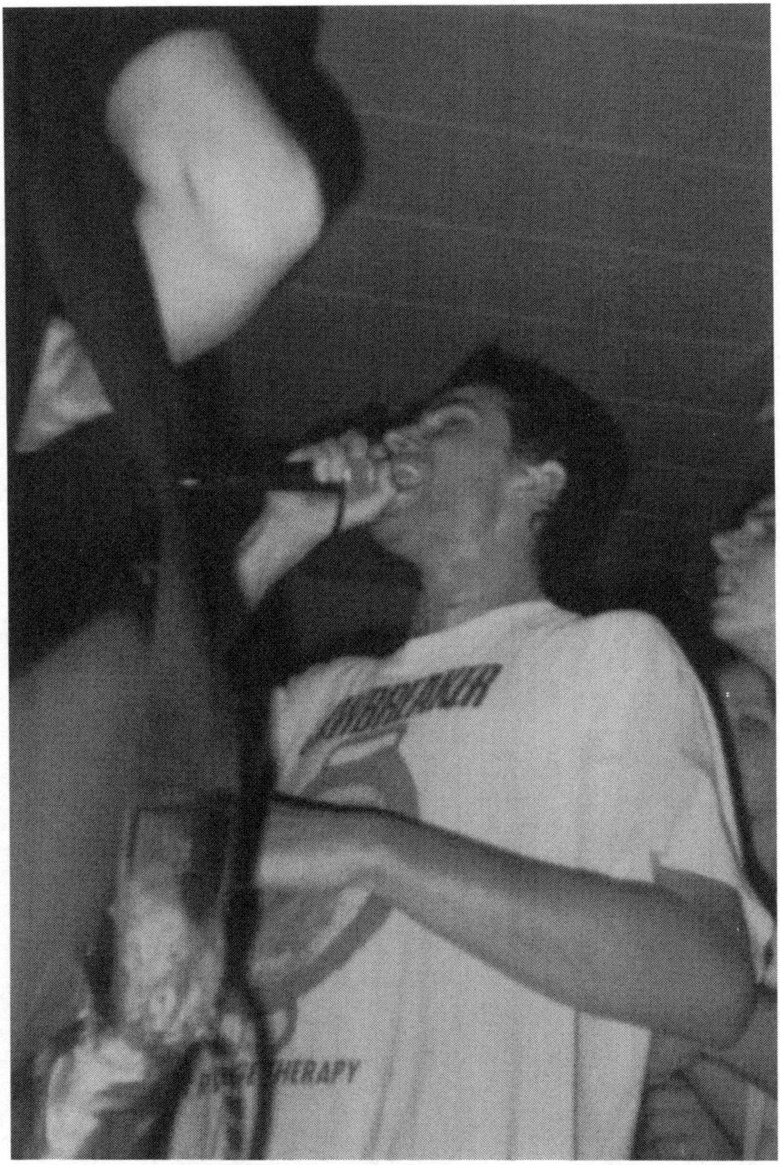

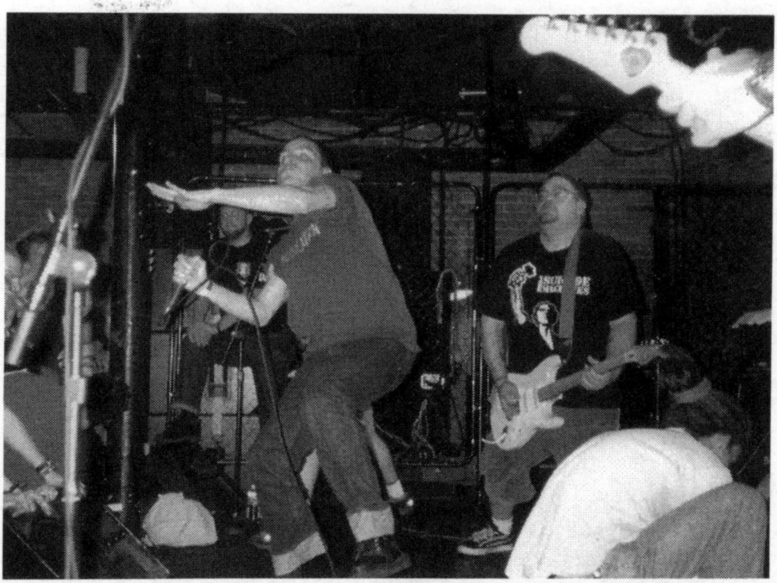

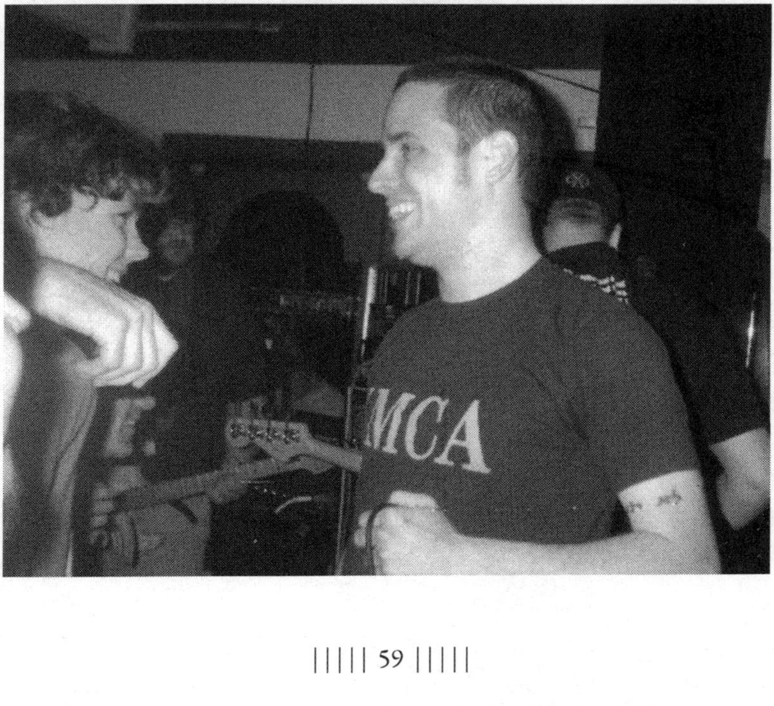
MCA

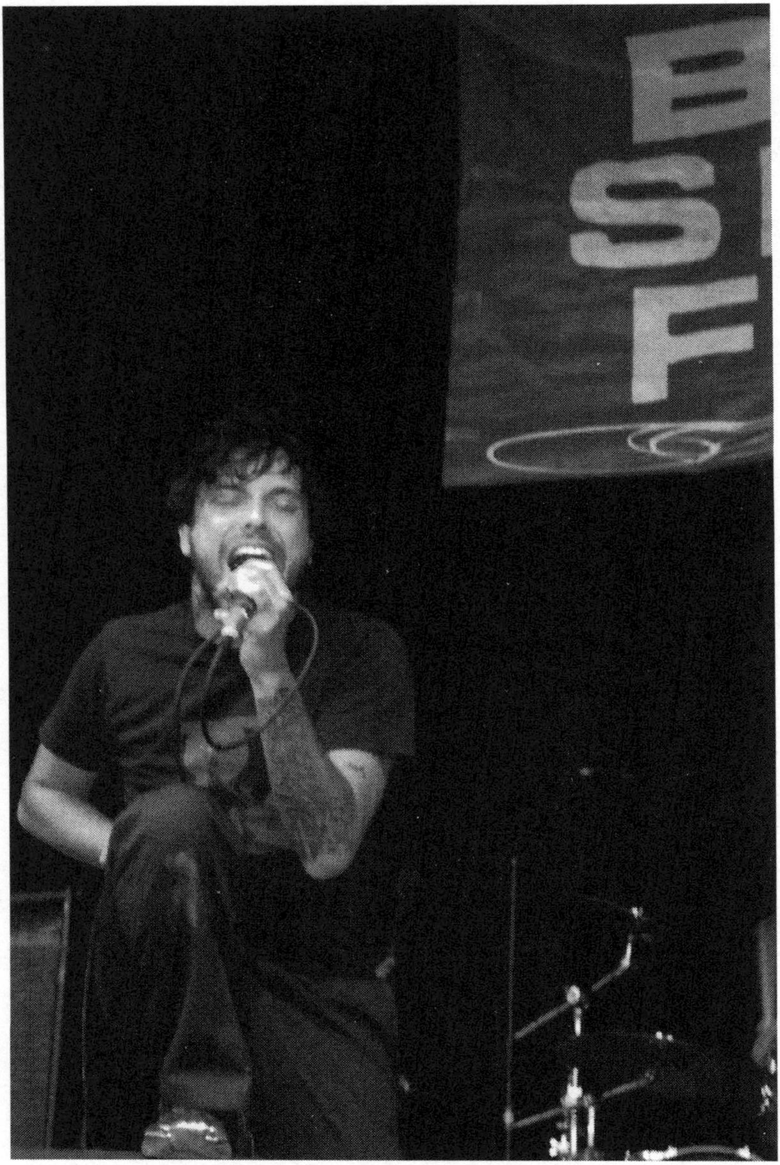

MOVEMENT II.

IV. DESIRE

*Did you give me desire just to watch me fall
'cause this pull is much stronger than your mission call*

**LEAD US NOT INTO TEMPTATION,
BUT DELIVER US FROM OURSELVES.**
    An arbitrary pilgrimage back to the Devil's Doorstep. 8 months 8 months 8 months mastering the art of self-destruction.
    Seeking solace in disasters.
    From couch to couch to floor to
    River Beds.
    Feed and Feed and Feed and Repent.
    The screaming is so fucking loud in my ears, I don't even realize that the sound is coming from my own throat.
    My throat, it aches
        raw with prayers falling upon deaf ears.

    But I WANT IT ALL. I. want. it. all.
    No resolution between "should be" and "am", I bury it deep.

    I'd pray for sleep if I was so humbled, a chance to wake and try this day, this week this life again.
    Wild eyes and the taste of liquor on a lovers lips. Faces are faces are ghosts. This mirror is clean and it's 4:00am, the snow white promise a lie -
    and here I sit, desperate for an escape from my escape.
    Pills... drink... where the fuck am I? Anywhere but there... anywhere but there...

Opening my guts for an empty room.

The waves are violent and I can't stop them -
I can't breathe I can't reason I can't find my feet
Only knees and a bus ticket.
The patriarch, my savior.

Sleep.

V. DAMASCUS

When in the stillness of the night I screamed your name
No shining light no not a word you never came
So I have come to lay these flowers at your grave / And move on in my name

FOR THE PROMISED LAND IS BARREN, AND ALONE WE SHALL WANDER

Achingly disenchanted.
Seeking solid ground upon greased tightropes as my afflictions were whipping into my spirit.

I am implosion.
Every single night a horror show -
No safety in daylight, when even in a room full of familiars my psyche choreographed an involuntary raising of the dead.
Pathological prayers still bleeding from my hysteric heart, no validation in presence or purpose of kingdoms earned or kingdoms raised.

There is nothing echoing back at my crying out,

Only terror and desolation.

Home.
Again.

The first few days back North with my parents were spent sleeping and recuperating my body. My mind was feeling completely out of control, but despite my exhaustion, I was relieved to be home and became a bit of a hermit for a while as I attempted to find my footing. It was no easy task. I desperately needed some stability but my synapses had other plans as they began to shudder under the weight of all that I was working so hard to keep tucked in. I became consumed by daily panic attacks; violent and without warning. I was 20 years old at the time and would find my way into my parents' room nearly every night, crippled by my anxiety, seeking their comfort and reassurance that I was not, in fact, dying right that very moment. They would pray over me and we would sit together until I came back to the ground and could attempt to sleep again. I don't think I felt rested for many years and took to sleeping in the afternoons when my body would eventually just give out. Always with the lights and TV on. I couldn't bear to be alone with my thoughts and had to be moving and occupied at all times. Anything to not be alone with my thoughts. Anything. Even now, I still require the comfort of a full plate and a certain bit of chaos to keep me sane.

There were never any outside triggers that I can recall to set me off. It was just like a sudden shock wave—my breathing would change and before I knew it, a full-blown domino effect of losing control would begin. I would feel almost outside of my body and I'd find myself wild and dizzy, in a bathroom mirror obsessively checking my pupils for signs of a stroke or pushing and pulling my cheeks for proof that I was even real. My heart, pounding loud in my ears, would somehow feel fast and slow all at the same time.

Hot and cold.
Hot and cold.
I am
Inside my body

>   and out.
>   I'm dying... I am dying.
>   I can't feel my face and my hands have
>   Disappeared.
>   The room is spinning and I
>   pray and pray and pray,
>   fast and terrified
>   begging to be relieved,
>   desperate to be saved.
>   My stomach, it's turning inside out
>   AndfuckIcantbreathe.

During every episode, I would be crying out for God to save my life, delirious and frenzied. I was absolutely terrified of death, and the fear was overwhelming. All consuming.

It was constant.

And I mean, constant.

And utterly exhausting. My raving prayers were so intense and filled with fear that I would often wear myself out with them and eventually fall asleep. Back then, I hadn't yet found a way to deal with the attacks, and The Drop would happen anywhere. I could be out with friends and it would slam into me, and I would think, "Fuck, I'm doing this in front of people" and I would do just that, completely unable to stop them. As the years passed, I learned how to slow them or cope with them, finding a bit of calm in showers or tossing on a hoodie, but there were several trips to the emergency room where after some monitoring, I would be sent on my way, assured that I would live to see another day.

Eventually, I moved out of my parents' house, needing my own space. After bouncing around and crashing with a few friends, I ended up in a place that was quite literally a closet, but it was my own. All that fit inside it was me, my cot, and my records. Not long after, I met a woman who I clung to as the source of that stability I so desperately needed. We got married after only dating a short time, and fairly soon after that, our son Simon was born. It was singlehandedly the scariest, most life changing, most amazing moment I had ever experienced. Born at home after his mother slaved through 28 hours of labor, he arrived into our lives on his own time, and so very loved. I remember holding him for the first time, feeling weak in the knees just thinking "Oh, God, I hope I don't mess this beautiful kid up!"

After he was born, I got two random jobs and worked day and night. I would often get in trouble at the more stringent of the two for spending far too much time locked in the bathroom, where I would go hide and ride out my panic attacks. Despite the good things going on, they were still pressing into my daily life with full intensity, where they would stay, a nuisance for many, many years. I do not doubt that they were intolerable for Simon's mother to handle at the time, especially with a baby to take care of as well.

I had been playing some music with a few guys in those days in a band called Nine, but feeling completely unfulfilled. No one seemed to want to put any passion into their music, preferring to sit around and write songs about drinking and women, content to never play a show outside of a 20-mile radius. It was frustrating because I desperately needed to be a part of something that I felt moved by, but I wasn't even close to getting it. I remember the breaking point for that band, and almost for my spirit in music itself, when I had written a song about something extremely personal to me and they turned it into a parody, and then recorded it and played it for me. My version was apparently "too deep" for their liking and they were making fun of me. I was pissed and felt extremely vulnerable... it was a horrible feeling. (One of them did later apologize for taking part in the mockery, which I was grateful for.) I immediately quit the band, and that was that.

Josh Latshaw and I, born just a week apart, have known each other since birth. Our parents had been friends at the time, and we even attended a Christian school together before my parents moved our family south. When we were kids, we hung out often and I remember him being stoked that we had white bread at our house, as opposed to the Roman Meal junk he had at home. Even as a grade-schooler, he was an avid guitar enthusiast, taking it up after he fell in love with the theme from *Dukes of Hazzard*. When I moved, we didn't keep in contact, and upon my return I found that as we had grown, we suddenly had little in common. (You know... in that punk kid kind of way where, to an outsider, you are all the same but within the umbrella term, there are a hundred different subsets. I mean, he liked Dead Kennedys, who I could not stand at the time, for fuck's sake. I think it had something to do with a beef between them and Agnostic Front. Yup, shit was no smarter back then.) We did eventually find ourselves together when I took on vocals for him in a band called Attic. We had a good time, until a falling out between Josh and I that was entirely my fault. I had moved in with my parents and sort of dropped off the face of the earth, just needing to get away and be a little reclusive for a while. He, rightfully so, brought in a new vocalist and changed the band name, but I was still livid. "How dare he just move on without me!" Unfortunately, this feud resulted in me missing out on his wedding, which I still regret to this day. When I began to return to the world, he and I made our peace and became friends again. Strangely, I remember our making up as being facilitated by the same singer I was replaced by. Funny how that works.

Two days after I left Nine in a fury after they had shit all over my lyrics, I got a phone call from Josh to ask if I was interested in playing with him and Chad, who had been sitting around on the porch that week, talking about starting a band. I readily agreed, and so began boysetsfire.

As a band, boysetsfire knew we wanted to play and see more than just our area. We wanted to travel and bring our show to wherever we could, and we began touring almost immediately. We got ahold of *Book Your Own Fuckin' Life*, grabbed an atlas and mapped our own tours, calling bands and venues to set up shows on the route we charted. It was so much different in those days. The community called the shots instead of promoters and booking agencies. We would always start with a hometown show in Newark, and go from there. One tour, we would play our way down south and back. The next, we would make the trek out west. Three- or four-week runs were the norm, and once we even played a month-long U.S. tour, came home for a day or two, and went to Europe for another six weeks. It was a lot of necessary work, sometimes less fruitful than others, but each night, when we began our set, nothing else mattered. It didn't matter that we were living out of a smelly van, wearing the same clothes night after night and sharing a loaf of bread and a jar of peanut butter between us. Playing was the reward. I remember playing everything from empty apartments to empty bars to empty fire halls. We played every show as if it were our last, and honestly with the way we were living… it probably could have been on any given night.

Another avenue that kept me occupied and outside of my thoughts at that time was the building of the Enoch Collective. The Enoch Collective was comprised of a small group of friends that worked together to put on shows in the area. It was all DIY, all non-profit, and very much about community. We booked mostly punk and hardcore shows, bringing in the occasional political speaker to rant into a microphone while we held our little fists in the air. Sometimes we'd collect stuff at the door on show nights like food for a local battered women's shelter. We paid our bands, hired security, hired sound, and booked the venues to play in. It was a lot of work, but a lot of fun at the same time. Boysetsfire often played the shows we put together, and it helped us grow ourselves in our scene, a self-making success story that not everyone was able to swallow their pride to congratulate us for, which was fine by us, really. The shows were a big draw back then, and we brought in bands like Bouncing Souls, Kiss It Goodbye, and Fugazi, who actually played the very last show we put on. At one point, it felt like we were putting together a show a week, and things just got to be more drama and work than it was worth, so we put the Collective to rest. I was certainly bummed to see it go, but by its last breath, it no longer served a purpose.

That 90's DIY punk and hardcore scene we grew from will always hold a special place in my heart, and boysetsfire owes everything to that scene. That community welcomed every style of music, every sort of affiliation, and every new idea. We all worked together, and the relationships we maintained with other bands and the people who supported us made it possible for us to gain any traction at all. We wouldn't have fit in anywhere else, and I think that is what we all had in common. Everyone was different, but everyone belonged. Diversity was its strength, and you could just be yourself. I will always be grateful for that. We were perfect for that scene, and it was perfect for us. At the risk of sounding like a grumpy old man, kids making music in their own hometowns today will never have that experience. It was an amazing and beautiful entity, but it just doesn't exist anymore.

The first EP we wrote and recorded was *This Crying, This*

Screaming, My Voice Is Being Born. Somewhere in the middle of that process, we met Mike Warden of Conquer The World Records while on tour in Ypsilanti, MI. A handshake contract, it was a failure from the start. Mike was broke at the time and we funded the recording and mastering of that EP ourselves. His sole responsibility was to handle the cover art and its production, which he did by way of repurposing extra record jackets by other bands. After the first year post-release, he became more and more difficult to get in touch with, making it nearly impossible to get our hands on our own records, which we needed for selling on tour. He did absolutely nothing we agreed upon, yet when we announced that we were leaving, he got extremely weird and volatile, making threats to kill us by burning us alive in our van. Just crazy shit. We found out he was still selling our music and insisted he immediately cease sales, but he refused, claiming we were leaving him destitute. We spoke with other bands who had been screwed over by him, and began the Boycott Conquer The World movement to help keep others from getting themselves into the same situation. It was a mess. We didn't even want money for records sold, we just wanted him to stop making and selling them from there forward, but every time we turned around, we got word he was still producing and still selling. We were so frustrated and he would not budge. He even came to a show once and cried when we tried to discuss it. It was a sad display. Since we owned the rights to everything and had spent our own money making the album, we eventually turned it over to some friends, who released it under Magic Bullet Records a few years later. (Brent of Magic Bullet has been a great friend and partner since then, handling U.S. releases for I AM HERESY as well.)

After being rejected by damn near every hardcore label that mattered at the time, we had no idea where to go next. Then, after a basement show with The Enkindels, we met Andy Rich of Initial Records. Initial re-issued our already completed *Consider* 7-inch, which we had previously released ourselves, and because we were constantly writing, when they picked us up we were well into the creation of our first full-length album, *The Day The Sun Went Out*. We wrote that album, (as well as everything we made, up through *After The Eulogy*) in the basement of Matt's parents' home. Nick Rotundo, a long-time friend of ours, came into the picture to help produce that album, and it was a wonderful experience. Everything felt new. Being with a label that supported our growth and put in the work with us was a great feeling, but we were still trying to get used to the business end of things. We hated the word "merch" or "merchandise," instead referring to said items as "Peaches." It was silly, but felt less douchey. I'll never forget the first time we made $100 playing a show, we felt like fucking royalty. It was still important to us to maintain a DIY approach to as much of the process as possible, a value we hold dear, even now. We all worked together to create the covers on our own, and we just had fun with the booklet for *The Day The Sun Went Out*. (Initially, the cover we created was a solar eclipse, but we scrapped it for being too obvious in relation to the title itself.) We always preferred to throw in winking suggestion and people often took it far more seriously than it was meant. I suppose that is just the nature of art in general—everyone sees and hears what they want to. I still get a kick out of the photo inside of that booklet of the baby with the rifle, which is Jonah, Josh's son. Each page was different, and we really had little idea of what we were doing in a technical sense, but we wanted to do it on our own, and we were proud to have done so. Since then, we have been fortunate to be surrounded by loyal and talented friends who have always been eager to lend their talents to us, and it has made each release special. A community effort.

The band really started to pick up steam once that album came out. We had only been playing for about three years at that point, but we were touring both Europe and the U.S. and writing non-stop in our "down time," so it felt like 10 years had flown by. In our short time together, Initial Records was amazing about getting us out on the road and introducing our music to new crowds, and the name recognition helped to get us into better shows and festivals. Andy Rich put on Krazy Fest for several years, and we always had a great time playing that weekend. Our invitations to U.S. festivals though, slowed after what I assumed to be a bit of backlash for speaking our mind too often. It seemed as though the PC crowd always wanted to talk a big game, but were most often too scared to back it up with action. I remember one More Than Music festival in particular, when a woman in the crowd began freaking out, screaming that the musician who was currently speaking on stage had raped her. She was hysterical, inconsolable and completely losing it. In my head, all I could think was "OK, this girl is in bad shape right now, and someone needs to help her. Get her outside, something." It didn't matter to me if what she was saying was true or not, she was very clearly in need of some support. But that is not even remotely what she got. Instead, the man on stage screamed obscenities at her, after which point the crowd began to join in, in a sick display of mob justice. We were horrified. We weren't there to crucify anyone on either side, but we had always felt that it was on the scene to police itself, and make it safe and welcoming for everyone. She eventually ran out crying. When we took to the stage for our set, I felt moved to make a statement, saying something about how I wasn't accusing anyone of anything, but that our collective retaliation to and mishandling of the incident was wrong. It became this indescribable platform where people in the crowd began talking about their own stories, giving personal testimony to similar incidents that had happened to them. It was a natural progression that came out of a place where people just needed to talk and feel like other people were listening and understood. I saw absolutely nothing wrong with that. Rather than interrupt people's floortime who were obviously feeling relief in sharing their own pain, we decided not to play during our set time. It WAS the MORE than music festival after all, and I assumed that we were all there to share an experience we wouldn't find at any other type of show. I was proven partly wrong when several people got angry, namely the folks running the festival itself. We obviously came there wanting to play that day, but we felt like something more important took precedent and we were willing to put aside our time on stage for that. I recall at least one other band following our lead. I do not regret how it all played out and I hope that everyone who participated in shedding their anguish that day walked out a little lighter than when they came in.

When Simon was three, his mother and I divorced. Her leaving was absolutely justified, and in the end it was good for everyone that she did. I had no self-worth or confidence then, and was content to be poor and completely unmotivated to push me to be better. She both wanted and deserved more for her life. While a confusing and crazy time in my life, it was still good and we got a wonderful gift from it in Simon. She later ended up marrying an amazing man and I could not be happier for the life they've made for themselves. She and I were meant to be friends more than anything else, and to this day we have a great relationship, often getting our families together to visit.

Nearly right after the split, I met a woman who was most certainly wrong for me in every possible way, but in that place of my life I really didn't feel deserving of love or celebration, and I hungrily attached to whatever I perceived as safety and stability. She had just broken up with someone who wronged me in the not-so-distant past, and I admit that it sort of felt good to pay him back. It was a little boost for my sickeningly low self-esteem to feel like I was "winning." Because of that, I completely ignored the initial signs of how sadistic a person she was, not seeing the blood red flags that they were waving. A stridently self-professed Feminist, she was hellbent on taking the upper-hand and showing off the prize of my prostration to everyone around her. And I let her. I was just so dejected at this point that I let it happen. I allowed all kinds of horrible things in those three years, not a single one I look back to fondly. She made me hate myself as a man and as a human being, while she meticulously and gleefully worked to tear me down. It started out with small things, like me asking for food during a rather low point when I struggled to make ends meet, and her telling me, staunchly and proudly, "no" in front of her friends to prove that she had power over me. They would sit there and laugh together at me, her wearing her victory over me like a patch on a Girl Scout's vest. Another time, I just wanted to tell her about a great book I was reading, and she looked me in the eye and flatly said, "I don't care." She very much enjoyed watching me crumble by her hand. She also found great pleasure in making fun of me to my own friends while I was standing there, in a challenge to see if I would stand up to her, or if I would attempt to save face with them. It was all just sickening and I was too weak to stand up for myself. It was physically painful to hide my panic attacks from her, but there was no way I could let her see them and use them against me. It was a horrible time all around.

Things changed when she started to be very apparently annoyed by my role as a father. She never took much interest in my son, and would be bothered when I would spend time with him (time away from her control). It was the beginning of the end. Eventually, I ended up cheating on her one night, desperate for someone to make me feel worthy and good, and remind me that I deserved positive attention and affection. I do not regret doing that because her subsequent leaving was like a noose being cut from the neck. Our relationship did nothing but remove power when I really needed it, and it still infuriates me that I allowed that. I truly did. I was not a victim of abuse but a co-conspirator in the demise of my worth.

Because I was in a period of intense confusion about everything in my life, my faith, my purpose, and even my sexuality, I went through many, many changes in a short period of time after that relationship ended. I tested all the waters within reach, looking for answers in their waves. Despite the mayhem in the process, everything I did was productive in the way of bringing me to my answers, and I neither regret nor am ashamed of the paths I took to find them.

After *The Day The Sun Went Out* was released, people began to take notice of us across the globe. Enter Victory Records. If you've paid any attention to punk and hardcore in the last 25 years or so, you are familiar with the plight of many bands who found themselves in the clutches of Tony Brummel, and while we were no different, I, unlike many, do not feel sorry for myself for having been in such. I am, in hindsight, extremely thankful we were able to enter into a very rare one-off deal with them, which allowed us to keep moving without them weighing us down. At the time, we were just elated to have caught Victory's attention at all. They had many great bands on their roster and we felt that it would be a positive move forward for us to join forces with them. I think only Darrell, who was playing bass at the time, was conflicted about the union. A devout hardcore kid, he was most concerned with our image within the scene should we become one of Victory's bands. In the end, it became an Us vs. Him situation, and we ultimately kicked him out because of his resistance to get on board (among an assortment of other reasons not worth mentioning). Rob Avery replaced him, and some time around our signing with Victory, we got to work writing our next album.

After The Eulogy was the take-off album for us. No doubt about it. Our team, our friends, and our families pushed that album hard, because they loved and believed in it. We were seeing success on both continents with it, and something in those songs just clicked with people. The album itself was equal parts weird and accessible, and everyone seemed to find their own power within the songs. Playing them live grew into an intense experience we hadn't yet seen. The album is 16 years old now and playing those songs will STILL light up a crowd in seconds. Those songs, that spirit, and the time in which they were written created a perfect storm for the long-lasting success of *After The Eulogy*. People needed that album. I needed it. It allowed us a platform to be passionate, angry and heartbroken together. People struggling with their faith, people fighting their way out of abusive situations, people angry at the system, soldiers stuck in foreign lands, people needing a family, anyone facing a battle. We worked through it together, raging loud into the night and fighting back, in unison.

Being in boysetsfire gave me such a sense of purpose at that time in my life. Through ALL times of my life really, but most especially then when I needed to learn how to channel all of my emotion into creation. I think at the beginning of boysetsfire, I had a lot of unfocused anger and hurt. I was pissed at everything and trying to deal with the first stages of my falling out with

God, the ever-present Stigmata, and every fiber of confusion and heartbreak and ruin that came along with both. Because I was so into punk when it started, boysetsfire gave me a place to point that: politics. It felt good to be rebellious and so I lashed out at things that couldn't fight back, like the government. A lot of people connected with that, even more finding resonance when my personal struggle with religion really came into my lyrics. After a few years of touring, I realized the depth of the ripple our music was making in people's lives when fans would come up to me after shows and describe these awful situations they had been in or were going through, and expressing how what we were doing was helpful to them. As I trudged my way through my own burdens, it was incredibly powerful to know that my life art was helping people get out of their own shitty experiences quicker, and it helped me keep going. We were without a doubt saving each other, and I hope that if anyone reading this was one of those people, you truly understand that.

By way of exposure, I think our one album with Victory was beneficial. Really, I feel like with the team we had behind us, and the name of Victory, there was no way we could lose. But, like so many others, we never saw a dime from our success with it, and we never will. Tony was inarguably an asshole but we were unaffected by his taunting emails. They were just words on a screen and like I said before, I and my band signed ourselves into it, eager to collect on what became empty promises. I never even met Tony in person until years after our split from the label. What's done is done.

Our *After The Eulogy* tours across Europe were huge and ended up creating an extremely loyal fan-base there, a success we absolutely owe to one man: Gero Langisch. A Euro-based publicist and promoter, Gero worked non-stop and single handedly blew us up there. He absolutely killed it, working me to the bone by lining up several interviews a day for me and scheduling meet and greets before shows. It paid off in a big way and I am immensely thankful for his dedication. I know that a lot of our U.S. fans never really understood why we toured so much in Europe, but the simple fact is that our Euro fans were loyal. They showed up from the get-go and stayed with us through every release, passionately engaging at every show. They traveled to wherever we were landing and made every night an incredible experience. In America, we always had a great time but it felt like every time we released a new album, we had to rebuild our fan base. The cycle was hard. We would play six weeks of basement tours across the United States and barely anyone would come out. There was a small (but mighty) fan base here and we loved each and every one of them, but not enough for it to make sense for us to keep making the rounds across the country. Financially, it was better for us to spend our time away from our jobs and families in locations that made it beneficial. Aside from that, touring in and of itself is hard work. Not that we didn't (and don't) love it, because there is nothing like being on stage, performing our songs to crowds across the world but being on the road, playing night after night is hard on the body, mind, and spirit and no one wants to throw that energy into a nearly empty room.

    I think a lot of people are often curious about what life on the road is actually like for us. They have this image built up in their heads that it's like a Def Leppard or Mötley Crüe video. And while I have to assume that for some bands it is exactly that, for us it is much different and I honestly think that is a large part of how we have managed to be doing what we do for so long. The secret is that, behind the curtain, it's a whole lot less exciting than you would think. There is a lot of hurry-up-and-wait:

Get to the club. Unload gear. Soundcheck. Eat dinner. Wait for doors to open. Watch bands. Prepare for set. We definitely spend all of that downtime being pretty low-key. We often play tourist together during the day when time permits but at the venue, there's a lot of exercising, reading, playing games on our phones, calling home, and just shooting the shit with other bands. Even when we were younger and more apt to party, it never happened backstage, instead heading to a bar after the show or something like that. Backstage is where our stuff is, and is the place we like to reserve for just people involved in the show itself. Before we play, we like to clear the room of everyone but us and those last 15-20 minutes before we hit the stage are spent quietly getting our heads and bodies prepared to perform. It's typically a pretty calm atmosphere. As we walk out, we will always tell each other to have a great show, take a few deep breaths and then it's on. For some reason, we started a thing a few years back where we all kiss Chris Rakus, who shares bass duties with Robert, on the neck before we walk to the stage. So yeah... there you have it. Backstage life consists of playing Angry Birds and kissing each other on the neck. Total rock star shit.

Once we set foot on the stage though, it's 110% the entire show. The switch goes on, and it's every bit as exciting as the first time we ever played...

Transformation in sweat.
Rebirth through the purging flames that kindle into a raging fire!
I am an individual part of the pack, and we have come to celebrate a great working.
As the first note strikes, I become fixated on the present. On the

here and now-
on the Is To Be!
I am god of my domain and master of my creation.
Purging toxins and taking in fresh air, bleeding for only a moment, knowing full well that
I shall soon find healing. I look out and see members of my extended pack —
Snarling,
Frantic,
Ready for the feast and celebration.
It is the most beautiful thing I will ever witness.
Together we ravage our weaknesses, and tear down the barriers that dare stand in the way of our own personal knowledge of god, life, and nourishment.
We belong to a new realm — a new era. A new dawn!
Warriors of Dark Gospel and Self Defense!
Masters of our own destiny, we are the Wolves, Goats, Owls, and Serpents in a land of sheep and vultures.
The brilliant lights, the thunderous sounds, the torrid heat, the wild lust, and the frenzied joy...
We are bursting at the seams.
We are all together,
and all alone.

I do have my own tradition for after the show that is extremely important to me. Each night, once the last song ends, I always hop down to greet my fans. I know that not many people do that, and I think part of what separates us is that we have ALWAYS been very within reach of our fans. We talk with them, connect with them, and build friendships with them, and they have returned that attention with their loyalty. There are people that I see at shows even now that have been coming out since the beginning and I cannot even begin to describe how that makes me feel. Our fans are the only reason we get to do what we do. They quite literally put food on our table, spending their hard earned money on an hour or two with us, and I owe them every bit of appreciation so it is only natural that I make the time post-show to talk with them, sign autographs, and pose for photos. When people purchase a ticket to our shows, they count down the days for weeks, sometimes months before the event. If they have a terrible week at work or are having a rough time at home, attending a show of mine allows me the opportunity to help turn that around for them by giving them an amazing experience when I am on stage and a very personal experience off stage. I want to thank them and let them know that their dedication to me, to us, and what we do is important. THEY are important. If you attend a show of mine, know that if ever there is a time when I do not come to greet you afterwards, it is only because something is off, like I am feeling unwell. Otherwise, I vow to be out there to say hello for as long as possible, and if the club lights go down before we are done, we will simply take it outside. I need to connect with you just as much as you want to connect with me, and I very much look forward to continuing this ritual with you all, as the Nathan Gray Collective.

The first two European tours were miserable for me—jet lag completely kicked my ass. I remember one show when we were literally minutes from being on stage and the guys couldn't find me because I was still passed out in my pajamas on the bus, exhausted from the time change. Someone came and got me and I ran to the stage, and ended up performing... still in my pajamas. By now, I have it down to an exact science. I always try to sleep on the plane and then take a 1-2 hour nap when we get to where we are going. When I wake up, I drink a bunch of coffee and then try to get to bed that night at what would be a regular time in the U.S. Trying to maintain a sleep schedule not much different than the one I keep at home has been key for me.

When we travel Europe now, we are fortunate enough to be able to do so in amazing and comfortable buses. That, of course, was not always the case and I still think about one of those first tours when we were traveling by van and we all got extremely ill. We were sleeping for 12-hour stretches and were getting these horrible headaches, and we were certain that we all had a flu bug until we realized the van had an exhaust leak that was filling the inside of the vehicle with fumes, poisoning us mile by mile across the continent. While you learn a lot about yourself and your bandmates when you are sharing a confined space for days at a time, I can't say we were heartbroken to upgrade to bus life. These days, we always travel in a spectacular double-decker bus, which provides us all the comfort we could want. It offers a lounge space where we hang out and watch movies, a stocked kitchen, and comfortable private bunks to sleep in. There is an unspoken rule that the bus be treated with respect and care because it is our home away from home. We've had some amazing drivers over the years: Tommy, who is currently chauffeuring us across Europe, and previously, a great man named Martin, who would drive us when no one else would. (Previous members of the band were not as respectful of the bus as we are.) Martin is a great friend and still comes out to shows to see us play.

Because there are many of us and storage space is limited, packing light is super important. Our bunks, while comfortable, are small and the trailer is full of gear, so we can really only bring a couple of outfits and shower stuff with us. You learn to bring a set of clothes that you wear for shows only because, holy shit, do they get gross. Some but not all venues have places for us to wash clothes, which means you are sweating under hot lights for a couple of hours in something you might have to wear again the next night. We used to hang show clothes outside the bus when we went to bed, but someone stole my shirt off the hanger one night a couple of years ago. So weird. Now everything gets tossed in the trailer at night.

Boysetsfire has always made a point to hire friends for whatever we needed. It goes back to our DIY roots and is something that I have also been doing as Nathan Gray Collective. It works for us because there is a certain level of trust and mutual respect that comes with working with friends, and really, sharing our success with people we know and love is a great feeling. Even Robert, our bass player, started out as a guitar tech. His band was touring with us when we met and we asked him if he wanted to join us on the road. Later, when we needed to replace our bass player in the middle of a tour, we knew there was no better person to fill that space than him. I am of the utmost certainty that Robert is currently breathing a sigh of relief that I am not relaying the entire story of how this passing of the torch transpired but, trust me… it's incredibly funny, and if you dig hard enough, you just might find an interview about it. Chris Rakus, who handles bass for our U.S. shows, is a longtime friend of ours as well and we still pay him when we play European dates, despite the fact that he isn't there playing. We take care of our own and everyone is treated like family. Oise, our Tour Manager, has been with us since the beginning. It was like love at first sight with him and like a parent, he is tough with us but always has our best interests in mind. He has played many roles for boysetsfire and I AM HERESY over the years as manager, driver, crew, merch guy and friend. He's truly awful at his job and fucks things up constantly and I'm not even sure why we pay him. But... he handles us well when we complain and give him shit. We love him dearly and he loves us. Sylvi, our booking agent, has been with us forever. She started booking with a group called Destiny, and when she left, we begged her to continue booking us. Our road crew has always been amazing—Tom, Rolf, and Jappo (who is new but who we loved immediately) are everything from stage managers to roadies to techs. Kris, our merch guy who is so quiet and reserved, but so kind and funny, and Sean, our sound guy who makes sure we always sound killer. These people have been with us through thick and thin, and we would all give them the shirt off our backs. They are not employees, they are family and we genuinely could not do what we do without them.

I have a real respect for EVERYONE involved in our performances and I make it a point to show appreciation to all of them before the night begins—people running sound, the promoter, people who run our lights, bouncers—it's on *all* of us to make sure the show goes well. I want everyone involved to feel included and to know they are each an important part of the experience. I love looking out from the stage and catching bouncers singing along to our songs or seeing how proud the person looks who is masterfully lighting our stage to add to the ritual. It's a great feeling to be surrounded by people who love what they do and really want to be a part of something that, for a few hours, consumes people in the way that only live music can.

While performing certainly gave me an outlet, it didn't abate my panic attacks. I remember that during a few particularly scary ones in those days, I would call my dad and he would pray with me over the phone. He has an incredibly calming voice and I usually felt much more peaceful after we finished our prayers and

I began to come back down to earth. While deeply concerned, they didn't really understand the nature of the attacks and I have to assume that they thought, perhaps, I was locked in Spiritual Warfare as I was crying out for the Lord to save my life. I never really discussed it with them but my wonderful parents met me at the Emergency Room many times over the years, always without the slightest hesitation or question. I eventually started to turn to other temporary fixes for the anxiety. I partied quite a bit, finding that often, there was a bit of solace in being able to attribute what I was feeling to being high instead being garden-variety out of my goddamned mind. They were a distraction, always seeking out the ones that kept me busy as opposed to those that would shut me off and leave me to entertain my thoughts. Like everything else, it was a bit of that binge and purge behavior, where I dove into it intensely with both feet, but could shut it off when it stopped being fun. I was perfectly capable of functioning normally without them but often preferred not to. I was also diligent about hiding who I was at that time from Simon. I created a sort of protective bubble, and when it was him and I, it was just that. Nights he wasn't with me though, I would go crazy partying, just trying to lose myself in those things in order to function within my own mind. Days that we weren't rushing off to school, we would spend at the park or at this family fun center near us, where we would both climb up into a giant indoor playground, chasing each other through the plastic tunnels and over rope bridges. But once he would go back to his mother's house, it was game on again. It was truly exhausting to live out that dichotomy of being a mess myself while trying to protect my family from it, and I'm certainly not proud of it, but it is part of my story.

The band had arrived to a place where we were busier than ever. We were writing and touring constantly, and in those days,

I was living in a place we affectionately referred to as "The Big House." I think most of our friends lived in The Big House at one point or another and it was like this spot everyone stopped at to work out their issues before moving on to adult life. It was just one long, insane party... there were many days where you were stepping over people passed out on the floor to get to the kitchen, and I very clearly remember when 25 or 30 of us ran to the attic to hide from the fire chief because we'd had this bright idea to toss everything inside the house onto the lawn and set it on fire. I think that was the last blow-out for that house because we were burning things in celebration of having been politely asked to vacate our lease. (Can't imagine why.) I am fairly certain the flames from our fête could be seen for blocks. A few of us even got praying hands tattooed to commemorate the crazy life we were living, joking that it would be our only way to get into Heaven.

After the painful process with Victory, we felt we were in good hands with the next label that signed us on: Wind-up Records. While a somewhat more pleasant experience in comparison, it was an extremely trying time for us as a band while we worked through who we were and what we wanted to achieve together. Early on, Wind-up bought *After The Eulogy* from Victory and we got to work on our next album, *Tomorrow Come Today*. They brought us out to L.A., where they wined and dined us with apartments and a posh studio space, and we absolutely lived it up on our off time. In the studio, we worked with producer Dave Fortman, who we all really loved but was tasked with taking our songs and formatting them into radio-ready hits. Songs that translated to dollar signs for Wind-up. While not at all something we were stoked on, we still felt he was a good guy, doing what he was hired to do. We tried to play the game just enough to keep them happy, without losing ourselves in the process: "Yes we will wiggle this part into a verse/chorus format. But not this one. And, fuck no, you can't bring in a writer to write songs for us." I might have been able to still feel satisfied with the songs on that album had they not been further defiled by one Jay Baumgartner. Before end production, the songs were good but just not played in a boysetsfire kind of way. When Jay got his fat fingers on that album, he mixed it right into garbage. The songs were completely stripped of their magic and I cannot even listen to that album without feeling angry. It sounds like a synthesizer being played underwater. The only saving grace was that no matter how they were recorded, we could always play them live in the way we wanted. And we always have.

Around this same time, I started to notice changes within myself. I can't really say how I might have arrived to that place but small things would happen that made me realize I was growing into a new me—one less fearful. I would randomly notice that I hadn't prayed in like a week and it would genuinely take me by surprise. I would say to myself "Oh, shit! I gotta start doing that again!" and sometimes I would. Eventually I just didn't.

I had begun my walk away from my faith.

At first, I think I probably felt a little guilty about it, or more so fearful of the spiritual repercussions I would face for falling away. Then it became a bit of a challenge in that I was walking away and looking back, waiting to see if God would chase me down and bring me back home. But he didn't, and I felt put off, realizing that perhaps I was talking to no one at all. It began to stir up something dark and angry.

The Misery Index: Notes From The Plague Years was, hands down, the most difficult collection of songs to create thanks to a tumultuous writing process. But in the end, it was one of the most powerful albums we made. We were still with Wind Up Records at the time and, with good (albeit, selfish) intentions, they wanted us to produce a hit record. A Grammy winner. Because of that, we were under strict limitations and they had a lot of control over the process itself. That said, they didn't do anything to us that we didn't allow them to. Just the nature of the business beast and, really, it was yet another instance of being a co-conspirator in the demise of self-worth. A year into the writing of that album, we had more than grown weary of the turmoil and stress we were feeling and we decided there was just no way we could maintain that working relationship with Wind Up without affecting the quality of the album we wanted to write, or even the relationship between us as a band. Because they wanted that one hit song, we were under enormous pressure to create in a style that didn't feel true to us. Even Matt, our drummer at the time, was pushing hard to back us into a place the rest of us didn't want to be. We found ourselves trying to write just one song to please everyone so they would let us slide with all the others. (They even tried to convince us to re-write Rookie into a radio pop hit. No fucking way.) After a lengthy band meeting on the issue, I went to the label to talk it out, telling them that not only did we give them one hit song, but two in "Empire" and "The Misery Index." They disagreed and I asked that we be released from our commitment to them. They concurred that it wasn't working out and let us walk away, no questions asked. I will always be grateful to them for that.

As a band, we decided to go through and rebuild the songs back into what we had previously written ourselves (without the obnoxious verse/chorus radio format on every fucking song) and Equal Visions and Burning Heart agreed to put the album out for us. From beginning to end, it took us three entire years to write that album and I am fairly certain that had a lot to do with why our popularity started to die off in the United States. We turned down so many great tours because we were stuck in that process for so long, saying no to hitting the road with Thursday and a few other bands making waves at that time, and I really feel that not being able to maintain that consistency with the U.S. fans made it difficult for us to keep them interested.

Despite how much blood, sweat, anger and tears went into *Misery Index*, it is still one of my favorite albums. It was also an epic Swan Song. I know a lot of people didn't really understand the diversity within it at first, but that is what made the album so beautiful to me. When I come at writing, I always aim to make a cohesive soundtrack, not an album of random songs. I want it to be a connective journey with twists and turns, one that pulls and pushes the listener into every emotion possible. I was still in a confused place of life during the writing of that album and I think the lyrics certainly reflect that throughout the entire collection. At the time, I didn't know yet where I was going but knew that I was going somewhere life-changing. What came out of that were songs that definitely feel somewhat dark and beaten down as I struggled to stay true to myself through all these transitions. It felt like I was allowing others to dictate my life through all avenues: politics, record labels, relationships, religion. Every one of them taking pieces of what is mine alone and claiming ownership over me. So many of the songs off that album deal with the outside forces dictating things that I should have been doing myself.

> "If I'm unworthy it's you that brought me here
> I sacrificed so much just to let you own my fears"

"I'll just wait for my heart to break
and arise from ash, reborn, reborn"

> "You and me, we are more like sheep,
> forced to march crippled feet to the slaughter"

"How empty we've become
Restricted and ashamed,
We crave what they provide us,
So we'll never feel alone"

> "so place your fork to mouth, eat, consume,
> be proud of what I let you see
> cause we've made quite sure you can never leave"

"sex drugs and politics are fine—just remember
that we own you, we bought you,
and we'll sell you whenever we want to
we break your legs and you will thank us for the crutches"

    Where I landed during the writing of that album was in a place where I knew I wanted to be in control. I wanted to succeed or fail on my own and I wanted to define my own success. Success to me isn't winning a Grammy or being splashed all over the radio, it is doing things myself, my own way. It's less about the end result and more in how I got there, and how happy I am with myself when I get there. That holds true in all areas of my life. I didn't want to be told what to do by a label, by a political agenda, by a holy tome, or by any other human. I wanted to get where I was going by being my own driving force. I feel like I have achieved that and I see it in the presence of true friends and devoted fans who are there for me through every turn, and not only accept me for who I am but truly get me. There is no better feeling than knowing that what I do speaks to people and makes them want to be better versions of themselves. My legacy is not going to be in some award but because people believed in me as a person, because I led a life well lived.

I had reached a major fork in my road. I knew the life I wanted for myself, and where I was headed wasn't going to get me there at all. Everything seemed to be shifting all at once—some lights turning on, others flickering off. I didn't want to wait anymore. I wanted my glory and my version of heaven and my freedom to be exactly who I was, right then and there. Why should I submit and grovel for someone who not only didn't protect me, a "child of God," from unspeakable horrors, but in whose name those very afflictions were laid upon me?

I had work to do.

VI. SET UP

I've whispered holy sacrament
And I've screamed my throat raw waiting for deliverance

EACH STEP FURTHER FROM THE MYTH
BUT CLOSER TO FREEDOM

    We are uninspired because we are uninspiring
We are bored because we are fucking boring &
We are weak because we have chosen to give up.
    We are willfully ignorant for the sake of comfort.

There is a moment passing you by right now
      | you're going to reach for it |
It's terrifying,
    it's bigger than you,
    and it is going to turn around and beat you to a pulp.

You will cry for mercy, and it will be denied.
Every ache, every pain, every tear -
The loss of blood, the fear, the exhaustion
They will overwhelm and overpower you.
    But
You will fight with everything you have.
It is then, in that quiet moment...
Lying in a pool of your own blood and defeat.
    The choice.

    To find Strength when your legs are too weak to stand
    To Persevere when all hope is lost.

This is what defines us. Not the roller coaster of joy and struggle, but the times we are mauled by life. The times that would leave mere mortals begging for the cold quiet solace of the grave.
Those who say no.
Those who refuse to be taken so easily -
   Those who have become their own gods.
THEY HAVE SEEN THE FACE OF DEATH AND WITH A DEFIANT LAUGH SPIT IN HIS EYE.
YOU CAN'T HAVE ME, I'M NOT FUCKING DONE YET!

|||||

"Now I don't know what stopped Jesus Christ
From turning every hungry stone into bread
And I don't remember hearing how Moses reacted
When the innocent first born sons lay dead
Well, I guess God was a lot more demonstrative
Back when he flamboyantly parted the sea"
—"Don't Pray On Me" by Bad Religion

I very clearly remember hearing this song and these words being the beginning of the end for my faith. A track I'd heard hundreds of times before, it suddenly had new meaning for me once the scales had fallen from my eyes. I went back to my Bible and read through it again with new eyes, literally weeping.

Faith had unceremoniously stopped being something I needed. I realized that I hadn't been prayerful or filled with the holy spirit, or even loving towards Christ over the last couple of years, and none of it had mattered. No demons had rushed forth to make my ears bleed, no lightning had come from the sky to brand my flesh, no angels had appeared to walk me back to Jesus.

Nothing.

It was liberating and empowering to not feel rejected by a sky-daddy all the time. I no longer needed (or wanted) God or religion, and while I had decided who I wasn't, I was very unfulfilled not knowing who I WAS.

There was definitely a waxing and waning period of covering my emotional turmoil as I moved into a new phase of life. I was still dealing with my panic attacks with disturbing regularity, but for the most part, I had become very good at keeping them from the general public. I had already begun dating Katie, the woman who would later become my wife, and she certainly pushed through some incredibly intense episodes with me, making more than a couple of trips to the hospital. She desperately wanted to understand them and sought out calming ways to help me get through them. I had honestly just resolved myself to the fact that I would likely be living the rest of my life in this cycle. They were as everyday routine as brushing my teeth.

When boysetsfire announced the split post-*Misery Index*, I decided that it was time for me to do my own thing, and that it would be a much different project. I was sick of everything at that point. Politics had started to feel like the new religion to me: suffocatingly staunch with a sick need to kill the individual. In the beginning, I thought that we, the punks, were for freedom, liberty, and personal responsibility. Boysetsfire itself always had a left-leaning socialist way about it, although I found myself more in tune with Anarchism, despite the fact I never would've identified as an Anarchist per se. There seemed to have been this big shift that happened, during which counter-culture politics all started to be more about offering different chains to be bound by, instead of removing them all together. Somewhat ironically, as I am looking back on this, I am reminded of that punk kid blasting "Peace Sells" that I thought at one point was the epitome of cool.

I needed a break to re-evaluate what I believed, and what I discovered was that I no longer adhered to a party line. I was worn down from holding onto views that didn't hold water for me. Sick of being told that I wasn't allowed to step out of the box. Sick of having to toe the line or suffer a consequence. I refused to ever again allow anyone to tell me that I was wrong, dirty, sinful, stupid or weak, most especially not people who didn't even believe in sin itself. I would no longer downplay my individual thoughts for "groupthink."

That is when I began The Casting Out. Originally, it was supposed to be a solo project, but I ended up chickening out. (In retrospect, I'm glad it didn't pan out that way, because it made coming into my own as a solo artist years later even sweeter. By then, I had aligned all my stars and was in the right place of life and frame of mind for it to be strong and genuine.) What The Casting Out became, however, was a bit of a mess that reflected where I was at in that time of life: a drunken party with no real direction. The project was very unfulfilling and I was miserable during much of that time.

Restless, disillusioned, and somewhat angry, I went looking for new knowledge to feed myself. I had all these questions, and no real answers. After diving into what I could through some research on the Internet, I made my first important book purchase: *Godless* by Dan Barker. It was exactly the right book for me to start with because it came from a man who had lived a life not so different from mine, and I connected to it right away. Barker had gone from evangelical preacher to outspoken atheist, and had no qualms about the shift. I found a bit of strength in his fearlessness and it encouraged me to begin a real process of self-critical thought.

After that, my next purchase was *God Is Not Great* by Christopher Hitchens. By the time I got to this one, I was confused and a little upset, and I desperately needed the sharp wit and boldness that only he offered. It was truly a "Fuck, Yeah!" moment as I soaked up his wisdom on everything from the jape of miracles to religious sexual oppression. I was immediately hooked on the blunt honesty that he so expertly delivered. Hitchens' *Mortality* was another book I devoured. It is still one of the most powerful books I've ever read; often hard to read for its emotional value but so strong and earnest. The book details one of the most upfront atheists of our time as he takes his final walk through life, dying of cancer. (A tragedy he fully admits being partially responsible for, due to diet and lifestyle choices.) He held his convictions to the end, never wavering in his truth that when it was over, it was over. He wasn't going to an afterlife of clouds and cherubs, and he didn't stoop to using that as a comfortable blanket for the impending finale to his life. The book itself ends abruptly, which is the most bone-chilling and perfect exit I could have imagined for it. I absolutely recommend this book for its raw honesty.

As I moved through my studies, I felt nearly smug as I learned and accepted the truth of God's non-existence, confirming each of my quietly held suspicions. I gained wisdom and learned to be more self-analytical. It was the most empowered I had ever felt and learning to take control of myself, for myself, was exhilarating. In a welcome change, Katie was a willing and eager soundboard for all that I was learning and discovering in that time. I would be bursting to talk about the things I was reading and she would always take interest in them. She became a big fan of Dawkins' *The God Delusion,* which she would listen to on audio book on the way to and from work. When she would come home, we'd have these amazing conversations about what we'd learned that day. She came from a place of no real religious ties and so our similar outlook provided a great foundation for us to study together in those days.

In the midst of all this new wisdom, I would often go back to the Bible to look up certain passages, realizing how horrifying the book really was. It floored me that I didn't see it before. Why doesn't the rape, murder, abuse or general disgusting behavior in the name of God phase anyone? People are offering their children as sacrifice to appease rulers, entire nations are being wiped out for worshiping the "wrong" God. Flood. Famine. Plague. Dismembering. The list is disturbingly long. When it was taught to me as a child, it always seemed as if the horrors in the book are happening to people that are "bad," and I accepted these things on the premise that they had somehow deserved their punishments. I thought I was such a loving person, but how could I have been if I never once questioned these things? That's how dangerous indoctrination and manipulation is. And of course it must start young, when no one is strong enough to call bullshit.

While I recognized that I was indeed an atheist, I still needed to find a better fit for what encapsulated what I was beyond that. It felt somewhat self-defeating to say "I am an atheist," because it held a negative connotation to me. "I am a person who doesn't believe in XYZ" is great for many people but I knew it wasn't the whole of who and what I was... merely a jumping off point. I had read a lot about Humanism in the beginning, which seemed like the go-to for new atheists. I found it wildly similar to Christianity and was very turned off by the love-your-neighbor vibes and good guy badging. It wasn't at all self-focused and I didn't feel like I needed a belief system to tell me to be good. I think the default response to "I don't believe in a deity" is often "well, where do I get my morals now, then?" For me, they were just there, inherently. I knew "right" from "wrong." I knew that life is so finite, that there are no second chances, for me or for anyone I might wrong along the way. That knowledge was enough. I didn't need a doctrine to point that out for me.

Everything up until that point had both blocked me from who I had always been, AND helped point me to it. I wasted so much time and energy in keeping my true self at bay that I had to go through and systematically tear all those walls down to get to myself. I could not have been more excited to rip them down as I went through my last Big Binge.

This time, no purge or repentance would be necessary.

VII. ANTHEMIC HEARTS

Sins of the father or fault of a god that made it so
We are the children you let go

WHILE A NATION SLEEPS
IN OUR OWN KINGDOM - WE ARISE
Shed in synchronicity, a pulling into new skin. Deliberate and full of dark grace, out with the old, in with the
New
Life
New
Voice
My new two feet.
These roads paved with backbones and purpose,
Arise. Arise.
Kingdoms are built upon the hearts of the devoted, and the minds of the determined.

The Casting Out eventually (and thankfully) self-destructed. It represented a time in my life I was all too happy to put to rest and move on from. In that same year, there was some movement about boysetsfire getting together to make music again. Interestingly, the catalyst for rebirth was the same one that put us into a place of splitting to begin with.

It is no secret that there was discord between myself, the band, and our drummer Matt—a lot of the tension during the last few years before the break surrounded his presence. I think it's fair to say that his vision for the band was not at all in line with ours, and he was very strong-willed about his way being the best for all of us. We disagreed. During the writing of *Misery Index*, I realized there was just no way that he and I were going to be able to be in a band together.

When Matt came to everyone about getting boysetsfire moving again, it was a tough sell. I think I was the last to even consider the idea and I remember sitting down with him to try to talk it out, saying "you know, let's just have fun with it." Coming out of that stressful process of writing *Misery Index,* I really wanted to be able to create and play and do it for ourselves this time. I didn't want to go at it with this goal of being a huge radio rock band. He convinced me that it would be different this time around, and I agreed to give it another shot. But it wasn't different.

After a short reunion tour, (during which the firestorm was so intense Robert actually left the band) we attempted to get to work on some new songs but the strain just infiltrated everything and no matter what we did, it was like pushing against a brick wall. Nothing was going the way it was promised to have been. I had worked really hard over the previous couple of years to get to a place where I wasn't going to let other people rule over me. I was no longer going to waste my precious time being willfully unhappy by allowing any kind of outside forces to dictate my path. That included other musicians. With Robert gone, it became very clear that it was not going to work out with Matt, and we ended our working relationship with him. I would wager a bet that Matt will most likely agree with me in saying that it is best for us to not work together or even be friends for that matter. We are just not compatible.

Once we got past that frustrating time, it was like a fog had lifted and we were finally able to really get to work writing *While A Nation Sleeps*. Robert returned, and we ended up having an amazing time making that album. It was such a freeing feeling to be more creative and really enjoy the work. The new songs essentially wrote themselves and with Chad at the helm producing that album, it all worked together to become this beautiful manifestation of rebirth. We even went back and reclaimed some older songs that we were never able to bring to fruition due to all the in-fighting and gave them new life as well. We pushed ourselves, tried new things, and held fast to what has always worked for us. I think a great mark of our moving forward was being comfortable in the fact that we didn't need to adhere to what scene lines, party lines or pre-determined styles dictated: we just did what we liked. If it was good, we went with it. Even that guitar solo in "Altar of God"... completely out of left field for us, but it came out amazing. I absolutely love the whole atmosphere of that album.

The album and merch artwork reflected a new place for us as well. It was more mysterious and forward-thinking. It had no forced aesthetic, no red stars—just clean, strong symbolism that can hold meaning unique to everyone. No longer did we feel the pressure to be a "political" band, a label I don't think we ever really even wanted. We had always strived to be revolutionary over political. To be more personal than global. In our younger ways of thinking, we aimed to be what we thought would make us a commercial success. Often, we thought that meant magnifying certain messages that riled people up. As we matured, it didn't make sense to keep beating that dead horse. It wasn't who we were anymore, and to be honest, political sloganeering wasn't what made boysetsfire—it was the personality and relatability of the band, the lyrics, and the music.

For me, it was great to have the return of boysetsfire at this time in my life because it really felt like home. And during that period of self-realization and discovery, having that constant familiarity helped make me feel stronger. I was growing and learning so much about myself and seeing the entire world in new ways, both on the micro and macro level. I had eaten the forbidden fruit and I was now ravenous for all the strength and knowledge I could get my hands on. On that particular album, the song "Closure" is the best picture of where my head was at, and it was most certainly inspired by all of those people and things that had previously removed my power from me. Ritualistically shutting the door with that song was an incredible feeling. My panic attacks were beginning to be less frequent and I was able to cope with them better than ever before. Evidence of that was the transference in which night time had become a friend rather than foe. It became my creative church instead of a fearful prison.

One of the more blunt and straightforward songs on *While A Nation Sleeps* (or even up until that point at all) was "Heads Will Roll." In a direct response to radical Islamic atrocities happening across the modern world, I had had enough and was ready to speak up. I remember writing that piece and Robert being just extremely uncomfortable with the lyrics and content of the song. I made some changes in the wording which helped somewhat but I know he still had a hard time with it being on the album at all. I truly believe that his discomfort was from a very genuine place, in line with his own personal beliefs and of those around him, and so I was more than happy to work to find a middle ground on that song. It stayed with his requested changes because I had things I needed to say and I couldn't continue to stifle that.

I needed an outlet for my anger.

I had grown sick of the constant fight in my spirit, sick of being mindful of what I said, sick of reliving my own horror story, sick of feeling that I was the weird one for not wanting to live my life on my knees, sick of apologizes and sick of shame.

    I went to war with it all,
    and I wanted to fight.

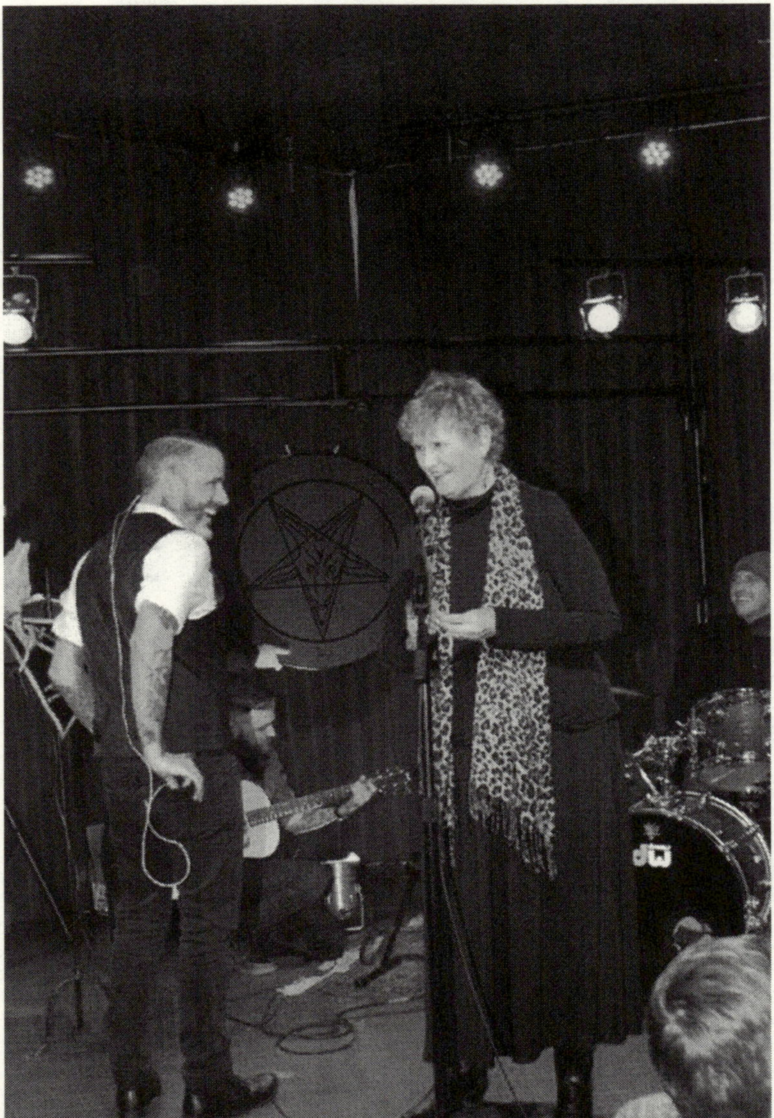

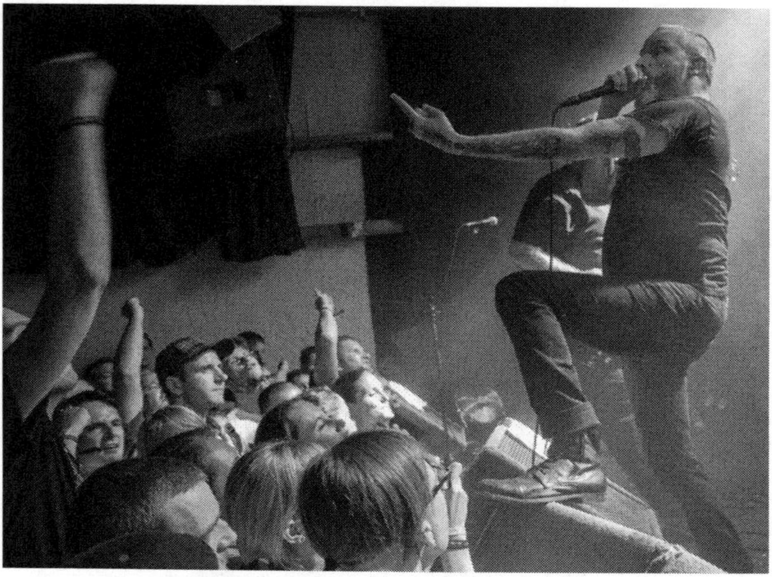

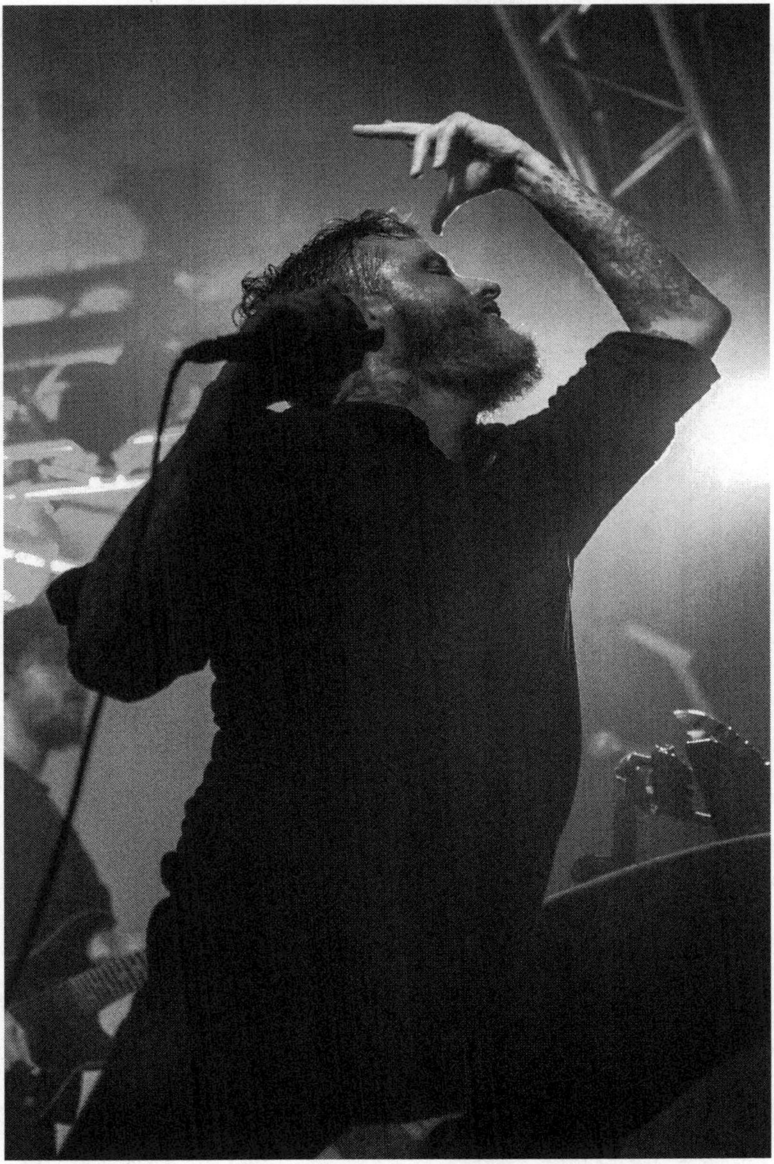

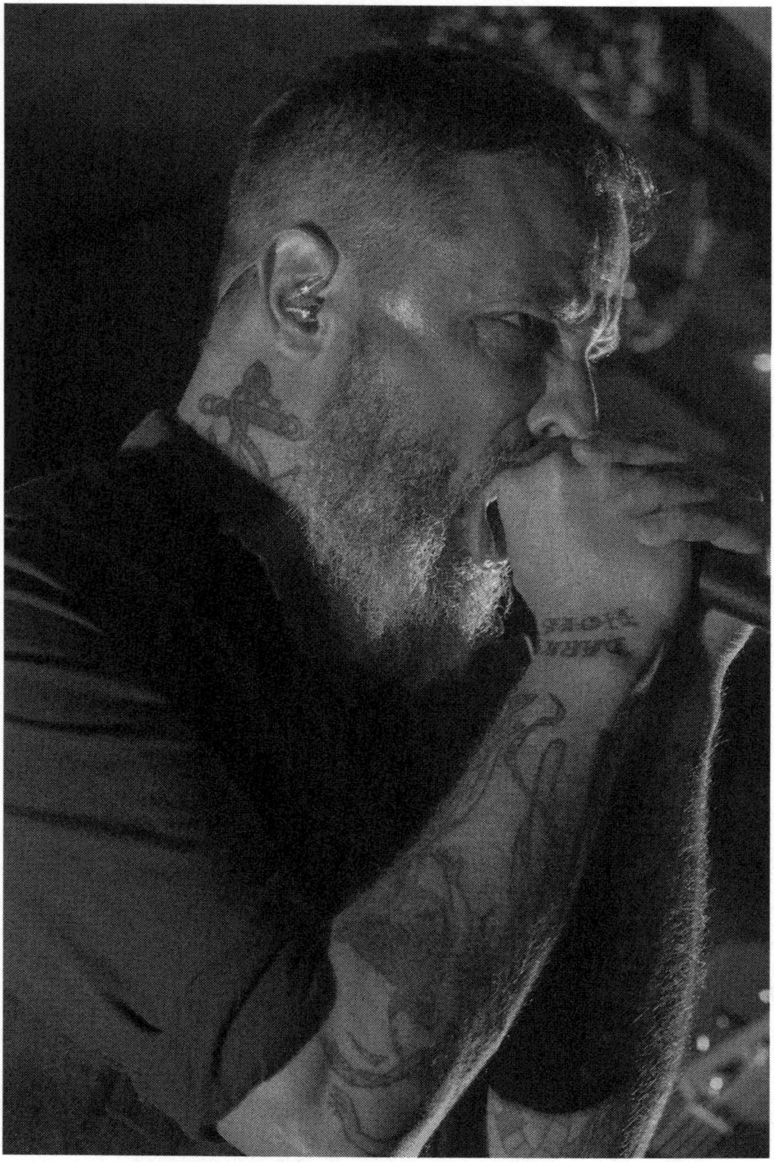

MOVEMENT III.

VIII. AT WAR

No time for contrition / Let the strong come alive
Burn down the empire / And take what's mine

WHERE THE DEATH OF GOD IS THE BIRTH OF HUMAN POTENTIAL.

Come and celebrate the beast inside you! Wear the skin of iniquity with your eyes wide open as you feed. Come forth, and devour all that stands against you!
Seek not to forgive.
Submit not to false love.
Rage! Destroy! Growl deep within your anger!
To repress your hate, is to fetishize it.

The most powerful thing I've ever done in my life was learn how to use my anger as a tool. When I began my journey with boysetsfire, my anger was unbridled and wild. I was directing it at all the wrong things and it was giving me no release. In fact, it did quite the opposite, just adding stones to the pressboard. This time was different because it was very self-aware and focused as fuck. It wasn't aimed at things that didn't directly impact my life, it was aimed at my own growth, and that alone.

I was enlightened but infuriated over having been lied to for so long.

I had been physically, emotionally and mentally scarred by religion under the name of a very intangible thing, and by a group who used a filthy, vile book as a weapon. Both were created just to keep me in submission, something no less ridiculous than the idea of Santa, (a farce people seem to be able to effortlessly grow out of at a very young age.) I was just fed the fuck up. Fed up with holy tomes that preached love while painting vivid images of death. Fed up that I, and no doubt millions of others, were forced to carry the weight of our Stigmata. Fed up that I had wasted so much of my life being afraid. Fed up with the idea that humans needed to be "taught" to be good. Fed up that people were slaughtering each other in the streets for worshiping the "wrong" god. Fed up that women and children were being bought and sold, raped, mutilated and tortured under religious laws that the State would not stand up to. It was disgustingly easy for people to use their ideology to inflict such atrocities, and I wanted to challenge the problem. I refused to stop questioning religion simply because it had become somewhat "politically incorrect."

In order to move on with my life, I needed to expel my anger and find my calm. I did that by bringing the Wolf out into the daylight with me, much like I had the Vampire. With the invocation of the Wolf, I found myself reclaiming my carnality with total abandon of shame and guilt. I allowed myself to be angry and to hate, and with those tools, I could symbolically kill all the things that had hurt me and be done with them. No more love thy neighbor bullshit. I didn't *have* to forgive a thousand wrongs, I could roll in my hatred and wear it like armor—hoisting it for battle, and putting it away victoriously when the war was over.

Through this exercising of my carnal beast, I began to accept and refine myself in new, more powerful ways. I was hungry for everything, sinking my teeth into book after book, song after song and just beautifully overwhelmed with artistic immersion. I learned how to entertain and exercise my carnality in ways I had never allowed myself to tap into. I learned there were terms for traits I had been carrying with me all along, but had been pushing down out of shame. I was voraciously delving into everything

I had, up until then, known as "forbidden." I decided to take control of things that used to be fear based for me: the monsters, the number 13 (which you will find repeating in several albums along the years), the occult, symbolism, demonology, and even Satanism. With that Wolf within, I was fulfilling empathy and reclaiming dignity. No longer would I be punished for who I inherently was.

Loving myself was my rebellion.

With that rage and confidence, I rendered each affliction powerless, and one by one they fell at my feet. Not through blind love but through concentrated hate. I torched that pile and made myself anew from the ashes.

I was ready to throw that energy into music.

I knew that in order to achieve that very specific catharsis, I was going to need to use a very specific catalyst. I envisioned an exceedingly dark, belligerent, angry sound—something I had never attempted before. It needed to be primal and raw.

I AM HERESY began rather nonchalantly, with my son Simon, his friend Jonah (son of Josh from boysetsfire) and I. When I first caught a listen of the two of them just messing around with their instruments, I felt a flame light up inside my chest — it was exactly the sort of style I was looking for. We sat down together and began to write some songs at home and then in the studio shortly after. It all came together very swiftly. And despite the fact that I was in this crossover time of The New Recruits, boysetsfire and the tail end of The Casting Out, I had no problem finding the time or energy to give I AM HERESY the attention it deserved. I genuinely needed it, and it was incredibly important to my journey.

Lyrically, it was the first time that I truly went all out, all in, stood completely defiant, and was completely unapologetic about my faith, or lack thereof. It felt amazing. Our first album, titled *I AM HERESY,* was an explosion of sound and emotion. The title track off that album (which was also on our demo from the previous year) is one of the most accurate pictures of where I was in that time of my journey: pissed off.

> Your gods are dead / We light the funeral pyre
> Your sun has set / We live for our desire
> A heretic / I'll be till I am gone
> I've kept my mouth shut now for way too fucking long
>
> Nothing above, nothing below
> The prophet's words have left you numb and cold
> Your sacrifice is dead and meaningless
> I refuse to bow down

I don't suppose many people were shocked to hear me spit lyrics out so vehemently, my falling away being more and more present over the last several albums from all bands I had been a part of. But, I do think many were surprised to hear such a lack of singing, which had been almost completely traded in for screaming. I had never used that style so much and so forcefully before then. I would often leave the stage and develop ocular migraines the second the adrenaline wore off. It was certainly a challenge physically but it was also the only way I could perform and reach the catharsis I was looking for.

Another track off that album that is hugely meaningful to

me and my journey is "And Yet It Moves." I fully admit that I had to actively keep my emotions in check when we recorded that song and whenever we played it live.

> My faith has been tested in the light of the inquisition flame
> My mind that you created has been possessed in your fucking name
>
> This is the city of the most high desperation
>
> I felt a burning, a burning in my soul
> A sense of violation, a sense of losing control
> Tearing twisting holy edict, power, lies
> Rewriting history, rewriting truth, rewriting lives
>
> You were never there for me
> And I blame you for everything (and yet it moves)
> This is the city of the most high desperation

A nod to Galileo, "And Yet It Moves" speaks to how religion turned on a man who otherwise had been nothing less than a revolutionary in the name of truth and science. Like him, I felt that I had given my all, only to be left out there alone in the end. I connected so deeply with how horrified he must've felt when the Inquisition came knocking on his door, dragging him into the streets for nothing more than presenting a case that perhaps the Bible was wrong about whether the Earth rotated around the sun. I genuinely got into and under the emotion of his story, the parallels shaking me deeply. I carried his betrayal as my own.

O DAY STAR, SON OF DAWN, (which was released the same year as *While A Nation Sleeps)* was this beautiful ode to Lucifer as the light-bringer. I was really connecting with dark symbolism and archetypes, and that album is a reflection of that in all ways. We had some lineup changes in the beginning of I AM HERESY's time, (Jonah eventually leaving to pursue a career he had his sights set on) but once it was locked in, I felt incredibly confident in the musicians we brought together. By the time we recorded *O DAY STAR* we were pushing through with our final lineup, which boasted three guitarists and each member was extremely talented and brought something unique to the table. Writing in that band was different than any I had been in before: Jay brought more of the chaotic sounds (think "Torch" from that album), Gregg brought in the rock vibe ("The Dawn of Errant Light"), breakdowns were Simon's gig ("Hive Mind"), and I was good at the off-kilter, dark synth and sound-based emotive segue (like "Tree of Knowledge"), Crumbs was an intensely solid drummer, and Matt played bass like no one I'd ever seen before. It all worked together incredibly. Looking back, I can definitely see the direct trajectory of those little off-beat songs I was so passionate about creating, which became the sort of music that inspired what I am now making as Nathan Gray Collective.

A few months before *O DAY STAR* was set to be released, I received some heartbreaking news about a longtime friend. Wauz Kenobi, a passionate, sincere punk kid I had met many years prior when his band, Red Tape Parade toured with both boysetsfire and The Casting Out, had been diagnosed with cancer. When I first met Wauz, he honestly freaked me out a little with his quiet and reserved nature. I never knew how to read him and it threw me for a loop. When I got to know him well, I realized that he was a rare and beautiful human. He was always very honest, incredibly sincere, and his brand of punk life was without a hint of PC self-importance. I loved him. We all loved him. He and Oise became extremely close friends and I will never forget a time during The Casting Out days when we had been invited to perform on an episode of a German soap opera. Simon was there, who had been a roadie for The Casting Out that tour, and Wauz and Oise came along as well, all three of them playing parts as extras. Wauz and Oise kept standing right in front of the cameras and kissing, just to goof off and get a laugh. It was such a random and fun experience, and something that still makes me laugh when I think back on it. Somewhere along the line, Wauz started dating Sylvi, our booking agent, and the two of them had a beautiful and loving union. We were all very happy to see them together.

Exactly one month after *O DAY STAR, SON OF DAWN* was released, and only four months after he was diagnosed with cancer, Wauz passed away. I am so thankful that I was able to visit him in the hospital before we lost him. Even when his body was weak with sickness, he remained the hilarious, warm, and genuinely kind man he had always been. I flew back to Germany a few weeks after he passed to attend his funeral, and that same night, shared guest vocals for Red Tape Parade as they played their last show ever in his honor. It was a beautiful and intensely emotional evening, and everything he deserved in celebration. He was a bright force in every single life he touched, and I often still play his song "Leap Year Of Faith," completely inspired by his declaration that "...some magic works."

I AM HERESY wrote quite a bit in our short time as a band, releasing music four years in a row, and as our sound developed, so did our stage show. I really wanted to create an intense atmosphere that would appeal to all senses in anyone who saw us play. It was important that we were creating a unique thing in which the stage, the crowd, and the space we shared became a ritual chamber—one full of both dark symbolism AND winking suggestion. Simon and I built an altar, Gregg was a wizard with the lighting, we had incense and sometimes candles burning from the stage, beautiful and fierce custom banners were raised stage left and right, and skulls were placed upon the altar itself. Total immersion. I hope to bring that to the solo endeavor in a different manner—dark with that solemn atmosphere, but in a very clean and almost debonair way.

Thy Will was the last album we put out and definitely the most intense. Rich with chaos and ritual, every track on it was an anthemic battle song celebrating the indulgence of the forbidden. We created an incredible video with the wonderfully talented Bobby Bates for the song "March Of Black Earth" and he perfectly captured exactly what we envisioned. I'm still very proud of that album, the video, and that time of emergence for myself. I had really begun to transform the Monsters into animal archetypes that I was drawing immense power from, and there was something new taking shape for me with that carnal family.

The fan reception to I AM HERESY was somewhat weird. People either loved us or were indifferent to us. No one knew how to categorize us. The metal purists were confused by us and they were, as a whole, resistant to what we were doing. I got the vibe that metal needed to be original, but only in the "correct way." I just don't think it was the right time for what we aimed to do and we had no immediate stability or growth. In hindsight, the slow build to create our fan base may have been due partly to boysetsfire having been reunited by the time I AM HERESY began to make some noise. Boysetsfire fans are, thankfully, extremely passionate and loyal. We started to get bored with the metal cliques around the time *THY WILL* was released and were looking at switching up the aesthetics and mood. But in the end, it sort of just fizzled out as careers and other interests demanded more time, a change I was vehemently resistant to. I was upset to see it end the way it did and I know that I pushed everyone hard to go all in on something that was perhaps not going to fly the way we wanted it to. But, I genuinely needed I AM HERESY during that time of my life and I think that as I look back at it all in the here and now, I can see that perhaps I AM HERESY wasn't really even meant for longevity. It was finite. And rightly so, because I would eventually need to get past that stage of anger and look forward to my future with a clear head and heart.

Despite its short run, I got a lot of good things out of I AM HERESY during my transformation. Those four years, fast and furious, were life-changing in all the best ways—I used my art to ritualistically break through the anger of my grieving process, I got to play music and travel the world with my first-born son, I challenged myself to perform in totally new ways, I recognized my true self after devouring a few very important books, I aligned myself with an organization that not only showed me that I was perfect as is but allowed me to celebrate everything I had been taught to hate, I began to focus my talents towards my long-term future, Katie and I were married in a beautiful private ceremony, later celebrated in grand fashion surrounded by our family and friends on an absolutely incredible night, and we welcomed the birth of our son Aleksander, who came into the world bright-eyed and full of wisdom, giving his mother hell on the way out but making up for it by being her very best friend.

Much like a fistfight, the I AM HERESY years ended with an adrenaline rush and a euphoric peace, and I felt full of pride at the throbbing pain in my fresh wounds, because they reminded me that I've just gone to battle, and won.

IX. REMAINS

*So here I stand here I believe
That I am free because I chose to be*

**I'D RATHER BE CONSIDERED IN LEAGUE WITH THE DEVIL,
THAN A SERVANT OF CHRIST.**

> Scales have fallen, and the flame is revealed.
> *I bow to no one.*
> *I AM CHAOS. I AM LOVE MEETS WAR.*
> Welcome, Master of Light and Magic.
> Father of Illumination.
>
> Welcome, Revelation.

During my time of reaching out to explore new things, there was a very definitive moment of self-realization that I will not soon forget. I had decided to go back to a forbidden little black book and re-read it with my new, fearless eyes. Anton LaVey's *The Satanic Bible* was like reading secret parts of myself written in another person's hand. I fed upon that book like a wild animal, reading it cover to cover in just a couple of days, nodding along elatedly in agreement. I realized that I was, and always had been, a Satanist. With its "The Devil helps those who helps themselves" approach to the world, I found in those pages my personal empowerment, acceptance and celebration. The book was a frank combination of fantasy, psychology, and logic that just... made sense. Immediately after I finished *The Satanic Bible,* I picked up *The Satanic Scriptures* by the Church of Satan's current High Priest, Peter H. Gilmore. I wholly credit that tome for being the solidifying piece of my puzzle. Reading the intelligent, practical, and pragmatic essays by Gilmore, an incredibly gifted wordsmith, made me feel truly at home. I was very much drawn to the "normalcy" of his implementation of the Satanic ideals. They were very life-applicable, and both inspired and championed the individual.

Because Satanism isn't about proselytization, and because this is a book about me—Nathan Gray: a man who just so happens to be a Satanist—I see no need to get into an extended essay of the philosophy itself or tread upon paths that have already been walked down and noted upon ad nauseum. If you are to know one thing about Satanism, however, know that it is not devil worship. Further, we do not believe in the existence of god OR devil. My personal understanding of Satanism encourages the individual Satanist to be the very best version of themselves. It encourages us to learn. Learn a trade. Learn something fun. To grow. To go into the world and make our own successes. Be self-empowered. To recognize that life itself is finite, and to strive for three things: to be happy, to be productive, and to do as little harm as possible to others. With other religions, people generally attach to them because they need them to make themselves better. In Satanism, you attach to it because you ARE better. We do these things by connecting to the archetype we feel strengthens us to do so: Satan. If you, reader, are interested to know more about the Church of Satan, I encourage you to seek out the answers for yourself. That said, for me, it makes more sense to talk about how I exist in a life well-lived, which is at the core incredibly Satanic. I would even go as far as to say that this entire book is a testament to the application of Satanism itself: a ritualistic piece of art that works to make me a better human. I do find it important to acknowledge my involvement with the Church of Satan and to clear up any misunderstandings that may stem from it but, outside of that, I adhere strictly to the brilliantly crafted lyrics of the *Diff'rent Strokes* theme song... Go ahead, look it up. I'll wait.

After burning myself down to the ground and finding my path at the perfect moment, I have grown to forge an incredibly solid vital existence for myself. My own ideals have flourished, my gifts have been refined, and while I know that I am forever a work in progress, I take pride in knowing that each day I am a better man than I was the day before. I don't need to be angry anymore. I am not crippled by fear. I pushed through those parts of my process, and on the other side, accepted that no longer did I have a need for a god to do for me what I could do for myself.

My god is me.

I am the sole creator of my destiny, and my luck.

Once I recognized my true self, I was ready to live deep within it. I had no desire to keep who I was under wraps and decided firmly to be exactly who I was. I wanted to show my colors. I was proud to have arrived to a place of personal power and I felt it only fair to myself to speak freely about my affiliation until I got completely comfortable, after which point, it became more of a natural thing to either talk or NOT talk about it. People will always ask questions if they are curious and I am always more than happy to answer. That said, I have always maintained that Satanism is a very personal ideology that asserts itself when necessary but mostly calls for its members to mind their own business. This, of course, makes it very easy to get along with others who stick to the same viewpoint. I may not agree with your personal spirit guide but I have no need or desire to convert you or punish you for your choice. I seek respect for my right to believe the way I do and to speak my mind, and I return the same respect to others. As a Reverend and a representative of the Church of Satan, I do enjoy the occasional opportunity to publically clear up misconceptions when asked or when appropriate. That trusted task is important to me, as it allows me to help define where Satanism is headed, and I get to help push the philosophy itself where it is meant to go. On those occasions, some people come away interested in knowing more and others are LESS interested. Either of those are perfectly fine by me.

I have, of course, been met with plenty of concerned friends, loving family members, and meddling strangers, all of whom worry about the penalty my heretical soul might face for my defiance. "...But what if you are wrong," they all ask. "What if this journey led you to happiness in this life but leads you straight to judgment and fiery torment in the next?" To that, I answer, "Then, so be it." Let your god prove my point by thrusting me headlong into the flames of Hell simply for calling his bluff. Let the sick sadist continue his eternal game of "Love Me... Or Else!" without me. Your god has not proven his worth to me and therefore has done nothing to earn or deserve my love and respect. *My* god has worked tirelessly to reinvent, restore, love, and care for me. My god will immediately answer my requests by rolling up his sleeves and getting to work on making things happen. MY GOD IS ME. "Cancel my subscription to the resurrection" as Jim Morrison said. Let the gods of white light and savagery hang on a tree built of the misery and suffering of those they mean to rule. They've been forever replaced by a much more credible source!

I know that some people were initially confused by my association with something so full of pomp and circumstance. I think they felt that it came out of left field for me, no pun intended. On the surface, they are partly right as some of the more fantasy driven parts of Satanism itself are not completely "me," but the fact is that Satanism goes much deeper than that. Ritual and aesthetics, while based on a common application, differ for each Satanist. We are a whole of individuals. As a kid, viewing the wicked films describing the dangers of Anton LaVey and his Satan, I absolutely connected to the capes, horns, and over-the-top rituals and aesthetics because it was fun fantasy. It was what initially piqued my interest, ironically working in direct contrast to the mission of those cautionary tales. (Those very things are also, thankfully, somewhat of a barrier, so to speak. Many people will never look past those eccentricities to get to the center of the philosophy itself.) I often quote one of my favorite verses from the Christian Bible when addressing the question of why I hold fast to something so surfacely peculiar, or how I resolve its flamboyant nature—*1 Corinthians 13:11* "When I was a child, I talked like a child, I thought like a child, I reasoned like a child. When I became a man, I put the ways of childhood behind me." I believe that it is entirely possible that I can be far more formidable by being an exceptional individual who is intelligent, well-spoken, powerful and successful than by simply being "spooky." Spook is mainstream. Spook is in. It is not enough to just look different, you must BE different. You must be extraordinary. I aim to complement my charming idiosyncrasies with strong foundations in work ethic. I dream bigger, I do more, I take command of everything in my path, and I will never stop being voracious. I have no time for bored. I have no need for boring. Because these personal attributes have always been how I've moved through the world,

I think that is what drew me to Gilmore's *Satanic Scriptures* so strongly—it was the real meat and potatoes of what Satanism is; more about the application of the philosophy, and less of the "Deviled Ham" as the organization refers to it. Currently, with the writing of my first solo full-length album nearly complete, I am injecting even more of that ideal into my music and its performance ritual.

Everyone is always curious how my devoutly religious parents accepted the news of my embracing a religion so wildly different from their own and from how they raised me. The simple truth is that my parents love me, as I love them, and we have a relationship that I recognize is very rare and unique.

My parents were married very young and have enjoyed a long life together, walking hand in hand down their road. Both committed themselves to their faith at young ages and they are partners in their quest to live a life enriched by religion, happy to continue bringing the word of God to those who want to listen. My maternal grandfather, the family Patriarch, was a gentle and loving man who not only raised my mother but was a father to my dad in the absence of his own. He was, like my parents, a very religious man and a staunch Republican. Anything but stereotypical, he taught us all how to listen to each other, how to be compassionate, and how to be genuine in love and respect. Some of my fondest, most cherished memories are of going to visit him, grabbing some sandwiches from the kitchen, and heading out back to sit under the gazebo and talk. Never one for simple small talk, our time would be spent in deep conversation about politics, religion, and the world in general. He loved to challenge and be challenged in the most respectful and educated way, and I will always hold those times with him close to my heart.

On his 80th birthday, we all gathered to eulogize him together, so that we could share with him how much he meant to us while he was still around to hear it. Eight years later at his funeral, in the most beautiful testament to the man he was, the speakers at the service all seemed to shine light upon the same parts of this incredible man. It was said over and again that my grandfather was a sage gentleman who made each person he met and interacted with feel like the most special, most important person in the entire room. He was never too busy for anyone. He always welcomed conversation and discourse with open ears. He never met an enemy and had a passion for life and the people in it like no one I've ever know.

Jesse Wyatt Wallace was an extraordinary man who passed down extraordinary traits. We all loved him dearly, and his passing left a huge void in our family.

Thanks to that inherited approach to life, my wonderful parents and I have always had a strong mutual respect for each other. I never had a "coming out" to them about being a Satanist. They just realized it the same way everyone else did and they never really approached the subject, knowing that if I wished to have a conversation about it, I would. And because they have never been anything less than loving towards me, I never feared they would think differently of me, berate me or negate my feelings. I, in turn, did not formally bring it up to them in a show of respect for their feelings. That said, nothing is too uncomfortable or too taboo to discuss in our family although, to be honest, we talk politics more than religion these days. (I think my dad gets a kick out of knowing that I've started to lean towards what some would call a more conservative standpoint on some issues as of late.) As a kid, they were always open to discussion about other belief systems but they were firm in their resolve, and I still had to go to church and I was still not allowed to play certain music in their home. These days, if my dad and I do approach the subject of our differing religions, often in a public forum like Facebook, he never puts me down or belittles my place. He instead takes the chance to affirm his own beliefs and why they are important to him.

On a smaller but equally as important scale, we respect each other's spaces. We often get together for family dinners, and at their house, we pray together before dinner. I will always take the hand of whomever is next to me and bow my head. At my house we just eat and they never insist upon or make a show of saying a prayer over the meal. They also never bat an eye at the decor in my home, which is mostly very clean, bright, and creative but does house a few skulls, sigils, and occult related items.

They admit they recognize the positive change in me over the last few years, even if they wouldn't want to attribute it to what it is: my study of and application of Satanism. I know that they are happy to see me find my stability, which has always been something they wished most for me, and are elated to see me comfortable with myself and maturing into a strong and productive man. I think they have been able to relax a little, knowing that I am going to be OK, and I am certain they are relieved to no longer be visiting me in Emergency Rooms.

If I could sum up my relationship with my parents on this subject in one single affirmation, it would be to tell you about the time my beautiful, God-fearing, wonderful mother took to the stage, stood at the microphone in front of a giant, custom Sigil of Baphomet, (the visual encapsulation of all that is Satanism) and warmly announced my band for the start of my very first show in my hometown as a solo artist.

My discovery of myself as a Satanist has been invaluable to my progress. No longer am I hindered by my past. No longer do I bear the weight of shame and fear. I am happy to report that even my previously ever-present panic attacks have all but completely stopped since I started to apply Satanism to my life. I genuinely believe that this is because I now know where I am supposed to be and I no longer feel trapped by negativity, confusion and uncertainty. There is an incomparable strength in finding who I am and living that out. These days, I am just trying to be myself, happily and unapologetically. I don't feel the need to continually announce or put out my affiliation because I am genuinely far too busy living an amazing life to have time to do so. That is how I am holding aloft my own Black Flame. That is the new era of me, AND of Satanism. I don't want the Church of Satan to be my "thing." I don't need them and they don't need me. But, I chose this association because I want to be here.

X. MEMENTO MORI

*In this hidden light we burn / We burn much brighter
Hold it close, and never let it go*

MAY MY EYES ALWAYS BE SET ON THE INFINITE, ANSWER-LESS, AND EXTRAORDINARY

Stanza Two
Like a race to defend my own relevance over and over.
Constant
Am I more afraid of dying, or of no one knowing I ever lived?
An impact must be made, or what was this all worth?
These are thoughts never had by a young man.
They are for those realizing mortality -
and stagnation.
Where do you go?
Where do you stay?
When is enough, and when is too soon?
May my eyes always be set on the infinite, answer-less, and
extraordinary.
All the days of my life, until death demands what is left.
Until life,
Is no longer a right.

"Remember death."
I have found that it is extremely rare to come across others that share my enthusiasm for mortality. An awkward and terrifying statement for most, within it I find peace and completion.

It moves me.
It inspires me.

It is an inescapable assurance, and my prime motivation.

I do not use skulls and morbid imagery in order to shock the masses or be obtusely morose. I use them as a reminder to not waste one single breath, or even dare to take the short time I have for granted.

I find beauty in sincerity and reverence in the knowledge of what I shall become.

Remember death.
Remember to live.

One day, we will be no more—all that will be left of what others knew of you will be dust and bone. When that day comes, what will you leave within your rubble? What legacy? What inspiration will arise from your ash?
I have pondered these questions and have found my answers within the ghosts of those lights that have gone out before me. Their legacy is in my hands. Their remains, a constant inspiration to never give up, and to never give in. I will not bow, placate, or tolerate ever again. I have seen the future, and it screams for us to stop wasting our here and now!
Moment by moment, we must give each minute the respect it truly deserves.
May my life be a constant anthem to wisdom, and every breath an ode to what is and what shall be. The inevitable is not mocked, and I will live in its reverence through joy and celebration in the here and now!

XI. UNTIL THE DARKNESS TAKES US

In absolution, our final resting place
In the stars once again

WE MUST REMEMBER THAT DEATH IS IMMINENT, IN ORDER TO LIVE FULLY, UNAPOLOGETIC, AND WITH FERVOR.
    TO KNOW THAT TIME IS BORROWED, IS THE GREAT MOTIVATOR.
    TO EMBRACE THE IMMINENCE OF DEATH, IS TO EMBRACE THE EMINENCE OF LIFE.
    While you control your path, the future is not dependent upon you.
    Time will move forward, and death is certain.

I do not fear death, because I have been death. I have had my hands within it, elbow deep in pain and misery, and I have reached within its throat and pulled out my own soul. I have shaken its stench from me and risen more brilliant than ever.

I am rebirth.

"...if you're frightened of dying and... and you're holding on, you'll see devils tearing your life away. But if you've made your peace, then the devils are really angels, freeing you from the earth. It's just a matter of how you look at it, that's all."
                                                —*Jacob's Ladder*

Coming to terms with my own mortality was a long, hard road. On this side of it all, I realize that it never even made sense to be fearful of death if I was supposedly going to the magical promised land of Heaven. When I accepted that there was no god outside of myself, and that there was no Heaven and there was no Hell, I found comfort in that lack of control. There was nothing left to fear.

> I will live. I will die.
> That is how the story will end.

I feel at peace in that chaos, stretching it over me and housing within its comfort. Immortality is what I seek now and I intend to achieve that by leaving behind something that transcends death. Immortality is in leaving a legacy. The reality is that no matter when it happens—when I actually die—I will leave unfinished work. Tomorrow. Next year. In thirty years… there is absolutely no getting around the fact that it will happen, and that I won't be ready when it does. So, it is extremely important for me to pace my passions. Not restrain them but focus them. Focus on what really matters. Focus more on my own happiness and less on the acceptance of others. Focus on my family, on my small but mighty wolfpack. On my music and my work. On all the things that bring me pleasure, and nothing less. My mark is going to be made not only in what I leave when I am gone but in how I lived while I was making it.

In my here and now, that is the work I have set out to do. I have relished the victory of overcoming every single thing that has stood in my way, including my own mind, which is often the most powerful enemy we face. To me, magic is the outsmarting, outwitting, overcoming, and adapting to my own thoughts and feelings. Self-doubt, fear of rejection, fear of the unknown… all things that hindered my advancement. It was not necessary for me to remove these feelings, as they continue to drive me to want to be better, but it was (and is) important to recognize and take control of them.

The power of darkness is immeasurable, and with a clear head and heart, it was time for me to move forward.

Making the leap into being a solo artist was something I had wanted for many years, but never really had the guts to do. At 42 years old, having lined up all my stars and shed the skin of my alleged iniquity, I was ready to push myself out of my comfort zone. Beyond that, I was ready to take total control. Being in bands like boysetsfire and I AM HERESY, I had the advantage of playing with a wall of sound all around me, my bandmates creating a bit of a safety-net in which I could put aside my nerves and take on that Vampire archetype to command the stage. Without that comfort, all I could see was a wild vulnerability. If it flopped, it was all on me. On the flip side—it WAS all on me. I wouldn't have to worry about the feelings, ideologies, opinions, goals, motivations or aspirations of others. I could do exactly as I wanted, in whatever manner I wished. That in and of itself was hugely motivating. It meant that I could play the style of music that spoke to me, and say the things that I wanted to say within it.

Once I had decided that the time was right to go solo, I knew one thing for certain—that it was not going to be me alone on stage with a guitar in my hands, playing folk rock under a single, lonely spotlight. If I was going to do it, it had to be true to who I was and where I was at. The music and the live shows had to be a collective, cathartic experience between myself and my audience, and it had to be rich in symbolism and raw emotion, all wrapped in aphotic sounds. They would be Abraxian Hymns for forward thinkers.

"Can I provide a common theme, belie the fear that is growing in me
Have I missed the mark 'cause I feel the strain
from growing old and starting over again
Let my life provide the questions let the answers some day come
Let my heart belong to this one moment if tomorrow never comes
Oh if tomorrow never comes

These worn out shoes have walked the line
This guitar my friend, is an enemy at times
Draws me to failure and reprieve
Draws me to this last wish before I leave
Let my life provide the questions let the answers some day come
Let my heart belong to this one moment if tomorrow never comes
Oh if tomorrow never comes

To somehow postpone the ending I'm so desperately pretending
To be relevant not the coward that I fear
So, let my life provide the questions let the answers some day come
Let my heart belong to this one moment if tomorrow never comes
Oh if tomorrow never comes"

I began writing at home, working to build my vision, and knew I needed to connect with someone who could help me bring that to fruition. I also knew exactly who that was going to be. Dan Smith had always been that friend who was doing his own thing—the industrial kid in a sea of punks. When we first met up to talk about the possibility of working together, I brought in some music that I was feeling inspired by and we sat down to listen. Most of what I played for him was neo-folk and I think he was a bit put off at first and will likely agree that after that first meeting, we were both a little unsure if we were a good fit for what I wanted to create. We came at it again with a "let's just try some stuff and see what happens" attitude and once we began to put some pieces together, it all just clicked. Dan is an insanely talented producer and working together has very much been a positive Hive Mind experience. He is able to give life to my ideas, hear things in ways that complement my own, and has an uncanny ability to envision the whole of the piece before I even complete my own train of thought. We are both quick to defend and stand firm on something we love, even if the other person remains unconvinced, but we always seem to come to a third side compromise and it comes out even better, every single time.

Very early into the solo endeavor, back when Dan and I had really just begun to put sounds together, there was a pivotal dream that broke through one night while I was on tour with boysetsfire for *While A Nation Sleeps*. It helped shape what became the Sigil of Nathan Gray Collective. The dream itself was packed with vivid imagery—dark and powerful, it was a total Jungian playground—and in the midst of it, a very clear collection of symbols presented itself. A couple of days later, with the dream still on my mind, I sketched out the symbols on the plane ride back to the U.S., merging them to create what became what I often refer to as the family crest.

Recording *NTHN GRY* was a great experience. Created in Dan's home studio, it was a very relaxed process and we felt free to try anything we could dream up. When we wanted to add extra elements to the songs, we would call upon friends and family members to lend their talents to the songs. I would often be struck with an idea and run to the guitar to play and record it on my phone, later bringing it to Dan where we would craft it into its full potential. In the same way, Dan began writing more and bringing his musical creations to me to add my personal touch. Everything just started to click. Releasing the EP itself, on the other hand, was an absolute whirlwind. We had been creating the songs in that space of "let's just see what happens," and approached putting them into the world much the same way. I was overwhelmed with emotions, and yet too busy to stop and let them take over, feeling extremely excited and somewhat nervous, but consumed with the task at hand—getting the music out there and seeing how people responded. I hoped that many of my most dedicated fans would be excited about what I was doing, but I knew that the style was much different than anything I had done before, so there was an uncertainty that I had to be mindful to not let overwhelm me. When we put that EP out into the world, dressed to the nines in a beautifully apocalyptic design with my sigil in stark white on the cover, we had no idea how well it would be received. Initially, we decided to just release it digitally on our own to test the waters. We could not have dreamed for a better welcoming... people were excited about it immediately and were begging for hard copies of the EP, and who were we to deny them?

I knew that I could have End Hits Records (boysetsfire's own label) put out the EP in Europe but didn't really have an idea of how to bring that to our American fans. Almost immediately,

Good Fight Music took interest in adding us to their roster after being introduced by mutual friends. A label that showcases hardcore, punk and metal bands, they brought us in and treated us like family, despite the fact that we were very clearly the odd man out as far as styles go. The Good Fight team is a great bunch of guys and Carl and Rick took a chance on us because they just genuinely liked us and liked what we were doing. I will always be grateful to them for that.

Our first European tour was huge for me in terms of solidifying that I was exactly where I was supposed to be. It was a wonderful experience all around and, honestly, just felt right. Chad came along to play drums and the three of us just meshed so well in our tour style, which was very important to me. We would play the shows and just hang out together in the van, watching movies and relaxing. It wasn't a high-strung, party experience. Just some friends making music and traveling Europe together. No pressure at all. The shows were so enjoyable for me and a completely different atmosphere than I was accustomed to. Between the songs themselves and the way we ritualistically approached the performance, it was a very intimate exchange of energy that was absolutely perfect for what I had envisioned. It was just an ideal experience in all ways, and while I had originally set out to somewhat sell myself as a solo artist, I was warmly welcomed at each and every show by many friends and familiar faces in the crowd. I continue to be incredibly thankful for everyone who has been so devoted to my work over the years, in whatever form it may take.

Near the tail end of that solo tour was an event that I am extremely proud of. Family First Festival was an idea boysetsfire dreamed up that ended up playing out beyond our wildest dreams. Over the last 20 years, we have been very successful in

Europe and we have enjoyed being a part of some incredible shows there along the way. Festivals are huge in Europe and we really wanted to try our hand at putting one together ourselves. We would choose the bands. We would choose the location. We would headline the event. We felt like boysetsfire was finally at a place where we could call the shots on something that huge, so we went all in on planning.

It was both exciting and a little nerve wracking to put together an event that big ourselves. If it crashed and burned, it would have been on us. On the flip side, being able to put together a show exactly how we wanted with musicians we knew and loved was a phenomenal feeling. One of the very first decisions we made during the planning was where we would host the festival itself. Köln has always been very dear to us. Even as far back as our first few trips abroad, the fans there have always been wonderful to us, and we can always count on having a great time with them. We absolutely consider Köln to be our home away from home and there was no better place to have that show. We booked Palladium Köln, a beautifully industrial and spacious venue that could hold up to 4,000 people, selected the bands that would share the stage with us, and began to promote the event.

Family First sold out almost immediately. And when we were able to release a few more tickets after so many heartbroken fans came to us about not being able to get one before it sold out, it sold out again. We even booked a pre-fest event at another venue to take place the day before, which hosted both boysetsfire *and* Nathan Gray Collective on the bill, and THAT sold out. It was just so overwhelming and intensely gratifying. The night of the big show was the one of the most rewarding and exhilarating experiences we've had together. People were lined around city blocks to get in several hours before the doors even opened. The

Palladium was well over capacity when we took the stage and when we looked out into the crowd, it was a sea of fans from front to back and up the sides. When they jumped and danced, it looked like waves creating across the floor. It was a very proud moment and one that will always be very dear to me.

As we were at work recording, releasing, and touring for the EP, my life outside the Collective was intensely busy as well. I think there was a definite shift in motivation at that time, having cleared my head and set my sights on that vital existence. On that immortality. I began an amazing new career that was extremely rewarding for me and kept (keeps!) me very busy, my local newspaper published a wonderful piece about me, as did a prominent magazine, Katie and I purchased our first home, (literal steps away from both Josh and Chad's houses) and boysetsfire made a couple of big European tours. Everything seemed to be happening at once and everything that was happening was utterly amazing. I was making my own luck and life was very, very good.

Not long after the digital release of *NTHN GRY*, boysetsfire began writing again as well.

The process of creating our self-titled album was unlike any we had gone through before. Essentially all of the writing was done online, where we would all create pieces and mail recorded elements back and forth to build the songs. I don't think we were ever all in one place at the same time during its creation. I recorded my vocals at Chad's house, where we would sit in his studio writing choruses together. That was also the first time we had written in such a manner and I genuinely enjoyed it. It was nice to not feel like I was writing in a vacuum and Chad is an exceptionally gifted musician overall, so his insight and ideas were always welcome. It was a super laid-back experience and I think that really shows throughout the entire album. Overall, I really think that album *feels* different from all the others. It definitely came together from a more mature and positive place, and really represented a growing into ourselves, encapsulating where we were at the time. Musically, the album *boysetsfire* was everything people knew to expect from us: big guitars, intense beats, and lyrics they want to sing along to. There were huge sounding anthems, some punk influenced tracks, some hardcore influenced tracks, and a lot of beautifully driving rhythms. But, instead of shining the light on all the negativity in the world, that album really focused on self-empowerment. Lyrically, it represented who and where I am in life, which is a place of complete comfortability. Because I had grown into myself, that of course changed how I view the world around me or, more specifically, my place in the world and how I celebrate myself within it. I am proud and excited to be who I am, and so the whole vibe of that album reflected that.

"I can't begin to understand the greater purpose
But I resign from making up a reason why
Our lives are short, and time unkind and I can't change the fear inside
Let me fall from grace
'Cause I will never be willing
I will no longer be willing
I will fall from grace
'Cause I will never be willing to stay quiet and in my place
I will no longer be willing to stay quiet and in my place"

Boysetsfire has worked incredibly hard for over 20 years now, and we have all enjoyed great successes from that band. Deciding what to name that particular album came very easily. *boysetsfire* is not only a statement of who we are, and where we are, but is really a celebration of the fruits of our labor. I think of all the albums we've made together, that is the one that really deserved to be self-titled. The album art was a very strong and clean white, with a beautiful golden serpent, which really could not have represented the mood of that album any better. Symbolism is very important to me and The Serpent itself represents our ability to create ourselves anew at any time. The Serpent is life healing. For me, music is the most perfect catalyst to achieve, and then celebrate that. That album in particular was a huge testament to growth and rebirth.

Just after the self-titled *boysetsfire* release, I took that energy and desideratum for rebirth, and pushed it forward into my solo project. Dan and I began writing the masterwork of my catharsis, steadily creating the first few pieces of *Until The Darkness Takes Us*. I had made such a phenomenal journey and I couldn't wait to document and celebrate that, song by song, in my very own way.

Writing took a bit of a back-seat however, when my beloved Grandmom fell at home, and was taken to the hospital. Somewhat inexplicably, though her age of 89 most likely at play, her health began to deteriorate while she was there. The first few days or so were full of ups and downs, as she would improve to the point where discharge was a consideration but then she would suddenly take a strange turn and begin to have new issues arise. Days became weeks and our family knew that she would likely not be returning home any time soon, if ever. So, we kept vigil.

Myra Brown Wallace, wife of the late Jesse, was an extremely important person to me. She was the most honest and genuine soul, always the gracious caregiver, and she was the absolute perfect partner for my grandfather. The love those two had for each other was sincerely of another world, and they enjoyed a beautiful 64 years in each other's arms. Where my Grandpop was inquisitive and analytical, always wanting to know all he could about those he interacted with in order to engage in real conversation, my Grandmom was a patient listener. You never felt as if she was just waiting for her turn to talk and she would charmingly but firmly chastise you should you interrupt her when she did speak. They honestly loved getting to know people and knew no enemies.

When she entered the hospital, it was early in the holiday season. A time when, not so many years before, we would have spent celebrating together in their home, singing, (at her insistence) "Thanks To God" in full around the piano before we were permitted to carve into the Thanksgiving turkey. Instead, that year we put up a small Christmas tree in her hospital room (which later came crashing down, shattering all of her ornaments when she got out of bed completely disoriented one evening, and fell into it. You cannot imagine how enraged and upset I was to walk in and find that. I recall screaming at caregivers for not keeping watch on her, tears streaming down my face.) You could not have forced me to leave her side during that time. I spent every possible hour I could in her room, needing to be near her and just utterly fucking distraught with the idea that I was going to lose this beautiful woman very soon. In the first couple of weeks, she too knew that her time was near. I think she was on a sort of mission to make sure each of us knew that we were loved and cared for, and she was very diligent about saying as much as she could before her mind slipped away from her. Her body was becoming more frail by the second and I will never forget the afternoon we sat together on her bed, my hands in hers, when she kept looking at me with these wide eyes and saying to me over and over again in a voice barely above a whisper, "I love you, always. I love you, always." It was as if she felt she couldn't stop repeating it until she was certain that I understood what she meant.

Her service to others came from a place of authentic compassion and was driven by her spirit as opposed to just her belief system. She would always find small ways to show love and concern—I even remember her mailing news clippings to my dad, stories of people who had been injured in motorcycle accidents after he purchased his first bike. She was very firm in her resolve but never needed to be rough with it, and never used it as a weapon. Religion was not something she simply participated in, it was who she was, through and through. When she kept telling me she loved me, she was letting me know that she was letting go of our spiritual differences. I know that she wished something different for me and was concerned about the future of my soul as a non-believer, but she also knew that the end of her life was coming fast and she needed to make sure I understood that she loved me—no matter what. I sat in that room with her, day after day, bowing my head in prayer with her when she needed it, singing to her (most specifically, that favorite hymn of hers, "Thanks To God") and telling her that I would see her soon. I wanted to do anything I could to show how much she meant to me and to help keep her calm as the transition was in motion. In what felt like just a day or two after she whispered her declaration to me, she became incoherent and was no longer the Grandmom we knew and loved. It was as if she had held onto her mental faculties just long enough to say what she needed to say to us all.

Still, I couldn't leave her. I hated being pulled from her bedside, feeling so guilty and heartbroken whenever I had to go. Boysetsfire actually had a show in Philadelphia during the middle of all of this, and Katie and I quite literally drove to the show straight from the hospital, arriving just before stage time, and leaving immediately after to return to her. That night, while I hated being away, was a very necessary break in the way of giving me a space to ritualistically work through all the anguish I was feeling. It was one of the last few shows we played in the United States, and surrounded by so many friends and family members, I pulled all the emotion I was carrying and worked it out in sweat and song. It was one of the many times in my life that I have felt incredibly grateful that my work and passion offers me opportunity to participate in a very unique and powerful form of therapy.

A couple of weeks later, I had just attempted to start returning to a normal routine when my mom called to say that Grandmom's caregivers felt that the end was very near. I spent the entire night in the hospital that night, and the next morning, was in my car on the way home to try to catch a quick nap before returning, when halfway through my short drive home, my mom called to tell me that Grandmom had passed away.

Her death, much like my grandfather's, was extremely hard for all of us. Mortality separated them for just a couple of years, but even in their passing, they were connected. My grandmother's funeral, held at the same place as my grandfather's, was attended by the same people, she was buried right alongside of him, and the sentiments surrounding the day were the same. My grandparents were the perfect reflection of love and grace. While looking through some notes I've kept over the years, I found a speech I had intended to deliver at my grandmother's funeral. At the time, I felt very moved to say these things out loud, but in the end I didn't utter a word of it and I'm glad I didn't. When it came time to speak, I remember being overtaken by the memories of the time we spent together while she was in the hospital and how disrespectful it would be of me to speak ill of the afterlife she found such great comfort in. I ended up tucking the prepared piece away and simply speaking from my heart about the joy she brought to the lives of everyone she knew.

While not appropriate for that time and place, I still feel that this short eulogy is my honest heart's desire still to this day:

I have not believed in a place called Heaven for quite some time. I say that honestly, and mean no disrespect towards those here who do.

That said, ever since the passing of my grandfather, and now my grandmother, his beautiful bride, I have not stopped wishing for it to be true. I have found myself desperately hoping that they should be given the honor of spending eternity in a heaven, together. I have never met two souls more deserving of what I've been told awaits us there, nor have I seen a love so complete for their God, their family, and each other.

As we lay my Grandmother to rest today beside my Grandfather, I am reminded what an honor It was to witness and take part in the lives of these incredible human beings.

Despite my inability to alter what I am sure to be true, it is my solemn wish today that I am somehow wrong... For I would gladly face judgement from a God I long ago disavowed, if I could do so knowing that Jesse and Myra Wallace sit beyond the Pearly Gates, hand in hand, able to continue their deep and abiding friendship for an eternity to come.

Moving forward, I was so grateful to have been able to have a time of closure with each of them before they died. I admit that their passing came with a bit of freedom for me in that I felt more able to be myself without worrying about inadvertently disrespecting them and their deeply held beliefs in the process. While the freedom to be myself is paramount, I am strong enough and loving enough to know that there is a time and place to exercise it out loud, and that is not simply "always." I hold dear the most precious memories of the two of them—my Grandpop telling us fantastic stories of his travels and time in the military, Grandmom in her adorable poinsettia shirt at Christmas time, seeing my newborn children in their arms, the way Katie would sit beside Grandmom, getting such a kick out of her special brand of humor, delivered nearly under her breath and dry as the Sahara, the glass cabinet full of dolls my grandfather collected from all over the world, those chats under the gazebo. There is nothing as special to me as family and I am fortunate enough to have had the most incredible people in mine. They are what inspires and moves me.

I very purposefully started this chapter with one of my favorite quotes. I truly feel like the application of that quote can used in so many situations, which makes it relatable to everyone in a uniquely personal way. "...But if you've made your peace, then the devils are really angels, freeing you from the earth. It's just a matter of how you look at it, that's all." I rose up to command my own devil-angels to let go. I have become so much more comfortable in my new skin. More relaxed. That positivity has very obviously spread to all aspects of my life, the impetus for all the success and vitality I could ever want. How do I know that? With the exception of the writing of *NTHN GRY* itself, everything mentioned in this chapter happened in one single year.

One.

XII. JETTISON

With my own hands I've forged these stones / To build a path through the unknown
With no more sins left to atone / A vibrant dawn of flesh and bone

ENRICHED ARE YOU WHO FORGE YOUR OWN PATH, FOR YOU WITHHOLD THE WISDOM WITHIN. TRUST IN YOURSELF, AND CELEBRATE THAT YOU ARE YOUR OWN GOD!

>Do we know what we are asking for?
>Do we know how to attain it?
>To become human
>To become a god.
>To understand our true nature.

Knowing our weakness and our strengths, and knowing how to celebrate them and work them both to our advantage is paramount. We must use them in synchronicity, until the lines between them become a blurred testament of self. The ego must thrive! That is how gods arise! Gods are not born by hiding, repressing, and shamefully denying themselves. Such nonsense is for the weak of will, and the poor of character. Why are we constantly looking for reasons to be ashamed of who we are? Why have we become so fucking afraid of ourselves?

>STAND
>THE
>FUCK
>UP!

If we are ever to heal and live again, this must end now. Find what you are great at, and conquer it. Find what you are poor at, and accept it. Stop wasting time! Jettison away what holds you back, and propel yourself ever forward into a life worth living!

| | | | |

There is rarely room to move forward without a bit of letting go. With the success of boysetsfire realized on our own terms, and the outward growth that set each of us on our own pathways for the future, I think we all felt that we were standing at a different precipice. Each of us had arrived to a unique place in the world and it was perhaps time to focus on our separate futures. We all had families, careers, hobbies and aspirations outside that band, and while we loved making music together, we ultimately decided that we all owed it to ourselves (and each other) to take a bit of a time-out to immerse ourselves into our individuality. In mid-2016, 22 years after Josh called me to ask if I wanted to jam, we announced that we would be taking an extended, indefinite break to pursue our own passions.

That summer, we made two tours across Europe. The first was a three week excursion, and the last was a four-date festival run. That festival tour was a completely perfect exit for us. We were treated to some massive crowds, full of many, many familiar faces that came out to say goodbye to us. We could not have asked for a farewell more full of love and intensity than we received at those shows. Our friends and fans showed us so much appreciation and the whole vibe of that last run was absolutely beautiful. One fan even wrote to the Nathan Gray Collective page to say that he could see how relaxed and happy we were. I think it felt so different than the shows before the last break because it wasn't at all clouded with frustration and chaos; we were all very much in the moment, enjoying our time together and with our fans. I am genuinely looking forward to building that same trust and relationship with my fans as the solo endeavor continues to develop. I aim to show them that my personal and professional rebirth was worth it, and I hope they walk into the new era along with me.

Out with a bang, we went, and I got right to work on completing my first full-length as Nathan Gray Collective.

There was a very prominent movement in my personal priority list that occurred after the decision to put boysetsfire on hold was made. Aside from focusing on the Nathan Gray Collective as a musician, I made a very intentional "cutting of the fat," so to speak, in which I would ensure that my full plate now consisted of only the most important things to me, and nothing else. If I was to live my life in the way I wanted, I was going to stop allowing myself to be pulled in directions that didn't directly benefit me. And while I've always been a master at turning that chaos into a meticulously crafted catalogue of successes, the time had come to do so on my terms, my way, for myself. I had to create homes for things that were mine alone, giving them space to move forward. This book, my music, my job, my home, my family, my dearest friends. These are the things that belong to me, and I to them, and together we all work towards building the future. Towards my dreams that I am slowly but surely bringing to fearless fruition. I am responsible for the creation of my destiny and it more than deserves my full attention. I cannot explain the joy and peace I feel on my weekends, painting, building, and renovating my beautiful home. Or the excitement I feel watching Aleksander grow and learn new things, and the pride I feel watching my Simon achieve his own life goals, one after another.

I cannot properly pen the words to tell you how anxious I am to meet my daughter who, as I write these words, is just weeks away from making her entrance into the world. I find great happiness in spending time in my own backyard with Katie and our closest friends, sitting around a fire and just talking until we tire out. I am inspired by the people around me and the places I have been, and I know that going forward, I am absolutely capable of anything I can dream up for myself. Relaxed and focused, that is exactly what I intend to do.

Writing the album *Until The Darkness Takes Us* has been vastly different than writing the EP. All avenues of my life had settled into the places they were meant to be by the time we began creating those hymns and a lot of the pressure I felt with the solo release had dissipated. I was really able to get outside of my head that time around and could just stop overthinking and release myself to making good music. And that is exactly what we did. As with most anything I create, the concept began with a spark of inspiration that just completely took over. Each of the 13 songs on that album played to very specific times in my journey, and completing them, one by one, has been an extremely cathartic undertaking.

| | | | |

Somewhere within the process of creating the album, I decided that it was time to push myself even further. Thus, the book was born. I really felt a need to tell my story and share it with anyone who wanted to listen. Part of me knew that this book, my autobiography, was the only way that I could complete my shedding with firm finality. Each chapter, digging vastly deeper into the guts of my pain, my joy, my love, my hate, my lust, and my victory. Releasing all that into the world will be my poetic expulsion, purging torments no longer welcome to occupy my heart and mind. From here out, my life will be an exercise of Warfare Through Celebration. Once I set my mind to the task, I immediately began writing, the words exploding out of my chest in waves, one after another after another. I couldn't get them out fast enough. Some days have been harder to push through than others as I confronted old wounds, but there was no fucking way I was giving up. I needed this, and I hoped that others would find a bit of solace in my story. I hoped that there would be even just one person who read it, and felt moved to take their future into their own hands.

If you are that person...please, if you take away nothing else from this book, let it be at least this:

You belong to yourself and no one else.
Never forget that.

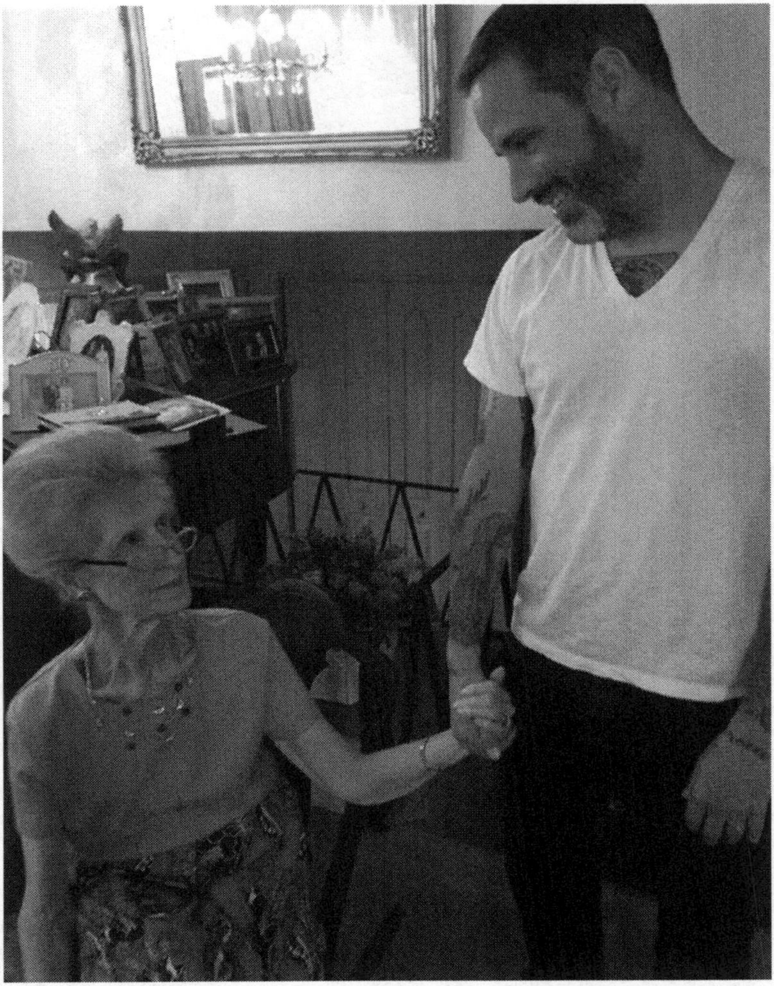

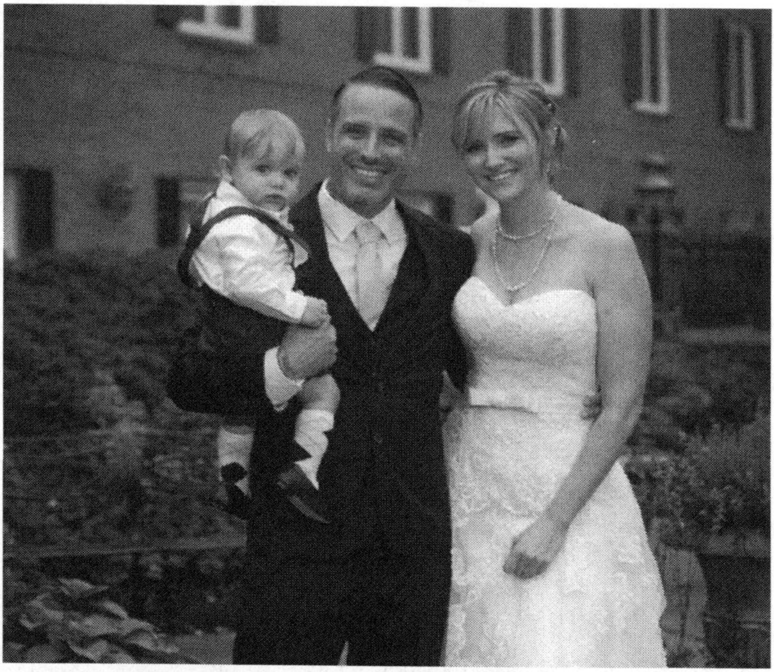

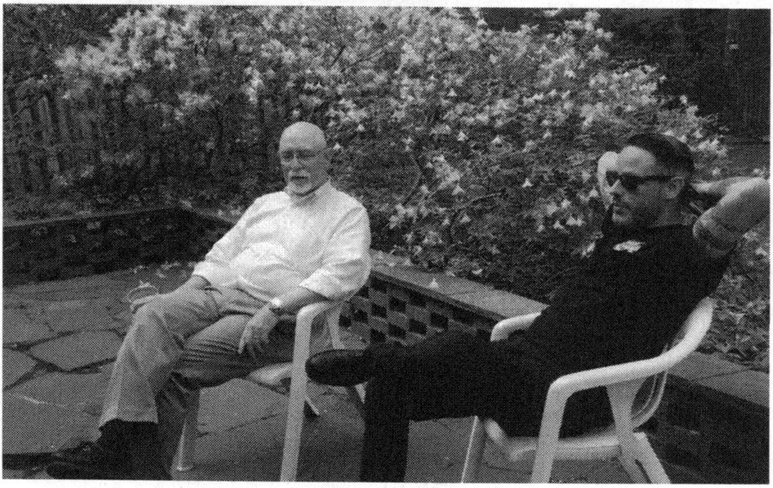

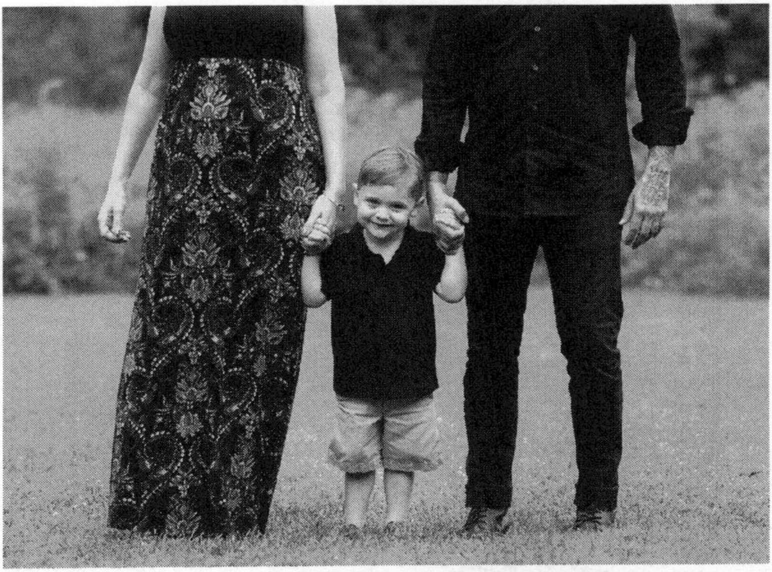

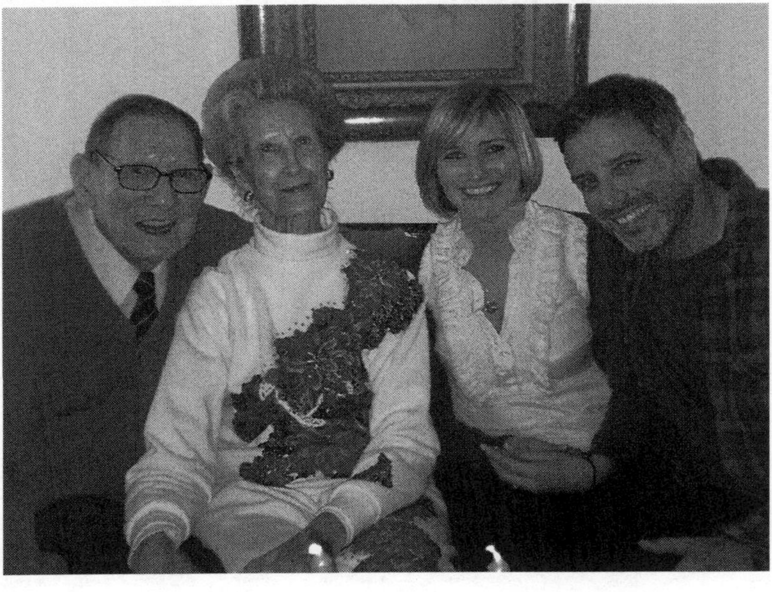

154

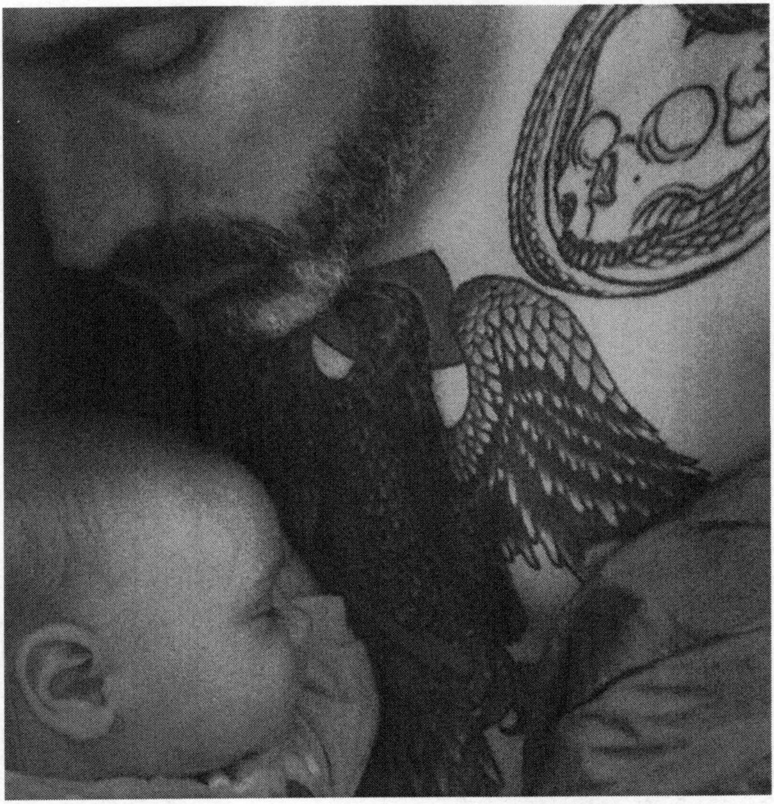

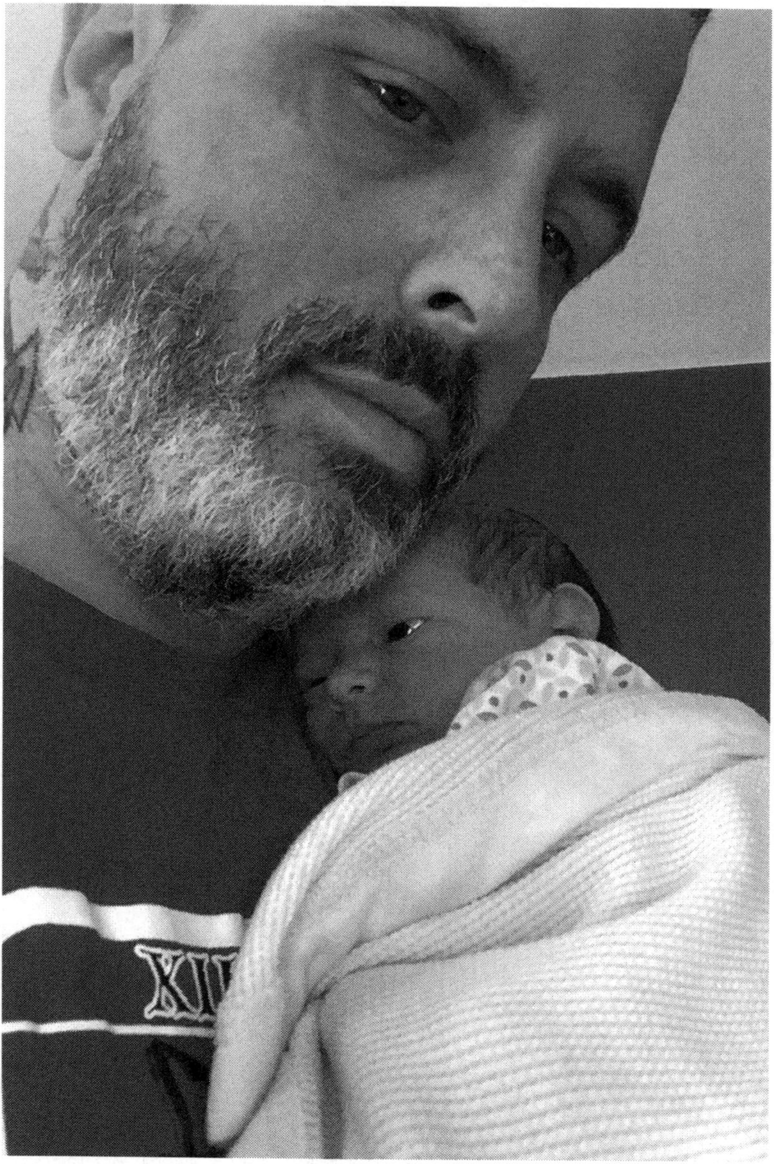

THE EPILOGUE

XIII. DARK FIRE

Fallen angels on the run / Lurid hunger wicked lust
We are savage and out of place / But in their shadows we found our way

AND FORWARD, WE WILL RISE!

Ladies and Gentlemen, I would like to propose a toast —

To the dreamers who fight for their dreams, unwilling to sleep their life away. To the sinners who refuse to let shame rule their very nature. To the men and women of true will and honor, who continue to struggle tooth and nail through the crushing uncertainty of life in order to provide for themselves and those they hold dear.
To the goat, the wolf, the owl, and the serpent living amongst sheep and vultures —
We are the future. We are the dawn of Dark Gospel and Self Defense!

May you take great pride in the path you have chosen, for it is a path that can truly be called your own.

I SUM INVICTUS... INDISSOLUBILI VOLUNTATEM!

"I went to the woods because I wished to live deliberately, to front only the essential facts of life, and see if I could not learn what it had to teach, and not, when I came to die, discover that I had not lived. I did not wish to live what was not life, living is so dear; nor did I wish to practise resignation, unless it was quite necessary. I wanted to live deep and suck out all the marrow of life, to live so sturdily and Spartan-like as to put to rout all that was not life, to cut a broad swath and shave close, to drive life into a corner, and reduce it to its lowest terms."

-Henry David Thoreau, Walden

I wrote this book as my Testimony — a testimony to finding myself instead of looking for an external source of strength. It has been a dark journey of self discovery and self deification, which ultimately led to fulfillment, self love, and joy in abundance. In the deepest shadows, I found that no one else would love me like I would, no one else should defend me like I should, and no one else could save me like I could. This book stands as the Dark Gospel by which to inspire those that are capable of being inspired. We are the Wolf, the Goat, the Serpent, and the Owl — infernal and carnal purveyors of self reliance, wisdom, rage, and lust.

WE! ARE! VITAL!

Sons and daughters of a new dawn—
A new era is upon us.

Let us embrace life by acknowledging the mortality that makes our lives truly "sacred." We are the poets of our chosen path, and the coming annihilation of all that would tell us that we are dirty, shameful, and unworthy. We are worthy because we fucking say we are! No god, no master, no hero, and no leader can give you that. It must come from within.

I sit here today writing to you as a free man. Take these words as you wish, and do with them as you will. You have read all parts of my story that I deem necessary to share, and if this provides you with hope, inspiration, and perspective, then so be it, and better so. These words are the anthem of my independence, and I have shared them in that same spirit. I stand unafraid of reprisal, criticism, or judgment, for I have done what is necessary for me to move forward.

To paraphrase a quote from the text at the beginning of this epilogue, *"I have resolved to live so sturdily and Spartan-like as to put to rout all that which is not life, for all that is not life, is surely death. We exist on borrowed time, my friends. We are promised no tomorrows."* We stand at the great precipice of the unknown. Those who have wisdom will continue to learn and adapt, to grow and succeed. Others will put their faith in some form of fresh-start ideology, and again, damn themselves to failure. There *are* no fresh starts in life—no new beginnings. Embrace your weaknesses and your strengths, know the difference between the two, learn from them, and grow!

Become you.

Your past isn't going anywhere, but your future may.
Become who you are, and stop living by what you are not.

life or death...
the choice is always ours.

APPENDIX

"Art, music, and philosophy are the great culmination of Greater and Lesser Magic, and the foundation for great war and great peace. It is what calls us to our own living ritual chamber, and beckons us to live!"

-Nathan Gray

MEDIA

Print
A Connecticut Yankee In King Arthur's Court - Mark Twain
Barrel Fever - David Sedaris
Crawling Chaos - H.P. Lovecraft
Fahrenheit 451 - Ray Bradbury
God Is Not Great - Christopher Hitchens
Godless - Dan Barker
"Invictus" - William Ernest Henley
Mortality - Christopher Hitchens
Paradise Lost - John Milton
Sex, Art, and American Culture - Camille Paglia
The God Delusion - Richard Dawkins
The Hitchhiker's Guide to the Galaxy - Douglas Adams
The Lucifer Principle - Howard Bloom
Walden - Henry David Thoreau

Film
Big Hero 6
Jaws
Labyrinth
Man of La Mancha
The Court Jester
The Dunwich Horror

Sounds
Against Me! - "Because Of The Shame"
Andrew Lloyd Webber - *Jesus Christ Superstar*
Andrew Lloyd Webber - *The Phantom of the Opera*

Andy Hull - "Back of Your Old Church"
Arcade Fire - "Intervention"
Black Flag - "Paralyzed"
Chelsea Wolfe - "Feral Love"
Christian Death - "Spiritual Cramp"
Danzig - "Mother"
David Bazan - "Fewer Broken Pieces"
David Bowie - "Space Oddity"
Death Cab For Cutie - "I Will Follow You Into The Dark"
Disney's *The Hunchback of Notre Dame* - "Hellfire"
Disney's *The Hunchback of Notre Dame* - "Out There"
Don Francisco - "Steeple Song"
Fable Cry - "The Good Doctor"
Fear - "The Mouth Don't Stop"
Iron Maiden - "The Number of the Beast"
Keith Green - "My Eyes Are Dry"
Leonard Cohen - "Hallelujah"
Megadeth - "Peace Sells"
Neutral Milk Hotel - "In The Aeroplane Over the Sea"
Nine Inch Nails - "Mr. Self Destruct"
Pedro The Lion - "Priests and Paramedics"
Peter Murphy - "Cuts You Up"
Petra - "This Means War!"
Philip Glass - *Dracula*
Pixies - "Break My Body"
Prince - "When Doves Cry"
Queensrÿche - "Spreading The Disease"
Stryper - "To Hell With The Devil"
The Carpenters - "We've Only Just Begun"
The Cramps - "Goo Goo Muck"
The Night Marchers - "And I Keep Holding On"
Undercover - "Where Can I Go"
Van Halen - "And The Cradle Will Rock"
Woods of Ypres - "Death Is Not an Exit"

SPARKS

"He therefore turned to mankind only with regret. His cathedral was enough for him. It was peopled with marble figures of kings, saints and bishops who at least did not laugh in his face and looked at him with only tranquillity and benevolence. The other statues, those of monsters and demons, had no hatred for him -- he resembled them too closely for that. It was rather the rest of mankind that they jeered at. The saints were his friends and blessed him; the monsters were his friends and kept watch over him. He would sometimes spend whole hours crouched before one of the statues in solitary conversation with it. If anyone came upon him then he would run away like a lover surprised during a serenade."

—Victor Hugo, *The Hunchback of Notre-Dame*

"No man knows till he experiences it, what it is like to feel his own life-blood drawn away into the woman he loves."

—Bram Stoker, *Dracula*

"How blessed are some people, whose lives have no fears, no dreads; to whom sleep is a blessing that comes nightly, and brings nothing but sweet dreams."

—Bram Stoker, *Dracula*

"And so you, like the others, would play your brains against mine. You would help these men to hunt me and frustrate me in my designs! You know now, and they know in part already, and will know in full before long, what it is to cross my path. They should have kept their energies for use closer to home. Whilst they played wits against me -- against me who commanded nations, and intrigued for them, and fought for them, hundreds of years before they were born -- I was countermining them. And you, their best beloved one, are now to me, flesh of my flesh; blood of my blood; kin of my kin; my bountiful wine-press for awhile; and shall later on be my companion and my helper. You shall be avenged in turn; for not one of them but shall minister to your needs. You have aided in thwarting me; now you shall come to my call."

—Bram Stoker, *Dracula*

"Under the strain of this continually impending doom and by the sleeplessness to which I now condemned myself, ay, even beyond what I had thought possible to man, I became, in my own person, a creature eaten up and emptied by fever, languidly weak both in body and mind, and solely occupied by one thought: the horror of my other self."

—Robert Louis Stevenson,
The Strange Case of Dr. Jekyll and Mr. Hyde

"It was on the moral side, and in my own person, that I learned to recognise the thorough and primitive duality of man; I saw that, of the two natures that contended in the field of my consciousness, even if I could rightly be said to be either, it was only because I was radically both; and from an early date, even before the course of my scientific discoveries had begun to suggest the most naked possibility of such a miracle, I had learned to dwell with pleasure, as a beloved daydream, on the thought of the separation of these elements. If each, I told myself, could be housed in separate identities, life would be relieved of all that was unbearable; the unjust might go his way, delivered from the aspirations and remorse of his more upright twin; and the just could walk steadfastly and securely on his upward path, doing the good things in which he found his pleasure, and no longer exposed to disgrace and penitence by the hands of this extraneous evil. It was the curse of mankind that these incongruous faggots were thus bound together—that in the agonised womb of consciousness, these polar twins should be continuously struggling. How, then were they dissociated?"

—Robert Louis Stevenson,
The Strange Case of Dr Jekyll and Mr Hyde

"Beware; for I am fearless, and therefore powerful."

—Mary Shelley, *Frankenstein*

"Even broken in spirit as he is, no one can feel more deeply than he does the beauties of nature. The starry sky, the sea, and every sight afforded by these wonderful regions, seems still to have the power of elevating his soul from earth. Such a man has a double existence: he may suffer misery, and be overwhelmed by disappointments; yet, when he has retired into himself, he will be like a celestial spirit that has a halo around him, within whose circle no grief or folly ventures."

—Mary Shelley, *Frankenstein*

"Satan has his companions, fellow-devils, to admire and encourage him; but I am solitary and detested."

—Mary Shelley, *Frankenstein*

"There are many who would like my time. I shun them. There are some who share my time. I am entertained by them. There are precious few who contribute to my time. I cherish them."

—Anton LaVey, *The Devil's Notebook*

"The strong man seeks out evil; the weak man is sought out by evil."

—Benjamin DeCasseres, "Under A Mask"

"Life in all its resiliency, beauty and strength is sometimes eclipsed by its unquestionable transient frailty. Today we are alive... tomorrow is not promised. And it seems, the evil that lurks in the shadows, this side of heaven, often has its say. But let it never be that we allow evil, which basks in our fear, to hinder our ability to live vibrantly unafraid of what tomorrow might bring. The only way to defeat the inevitable darkness that touches this world is to live and love brilliantly bright with purpose. To not do so, is to diminish the very memory and glow of all the beautiful lights that have gone out before us."

—Jason Versey, *A Walk with Prudence*

"The iconoclast proves enough when he proves by his blasphemy that this or that idol is defectively convincing - that at least one visitor to the shrine is left full of doubts. The liberation of the human mind has been best furthered by gay fellows who heaved dead cats into sanctuaries and then went roistering down the highways of the world, proving to all men that doubt, after all, was safe—that the god in the sanctuary was a fraud. One horse-laugh is worth ten-thousand syllogisms."

—H.L. Mencken

"The foundation of empire is art and science. Remove them or degrade them, and the empire is no more."

—William Blake

"Our ambition should be to rule ourselves, the true kingdom for each one of us; and true progress is to know more, and be more, and to do more."

—Oscar Wilde

"I have always felt friendly toward Satan. Of course that is ancestral; it must be in the blood, for I could not have originated it."

—*Autobiography of Mark Twain*

"If the truth shall kill them, let them die."

—Immanuel Kant

"Lest we forget at least an over the shoulder acknowledgment to the very first radical: from all our legends, mythology and history (and who is to know where mythology leaves off and history begins -- or which is which), the very first radical known to man who rebelled against the establishment and did it so effectively that he at least won his own kingdom—Lucifer."

—Saul D. Alinsky,
Rules for Radicals: A Pragmatic Primer for Realistic Radicals

OEUVRE

1994: Demo - boysetsfire
1995: *Premonition, Change, Revolt* - boysetsfire
1996: *Consider* - boysetsfire
1996: *This Crying, This Screaming, My Voice Is Being Born* - boysetsfire
1997: *The Day the Sun Went Out* - boysetsfire
1998: *In Chrysalis* - boysetsfire
1999: *Snapcase vs. Boysetsfire* (split)
2000: *Crush 'Em All Vol. 1* (Boysetsfire/Shai Hulud split)
2000: *Coalesce / Boysetsfire* (split)
2001: *Suckerpunch Training* - boysetsfire
2002: *Live for Today* - boysetsfire
2000: *After the Eulogy* - boysetsfire
2003: *Tomorrow Come Today* - boysetsfire
2003: *Last Year's Nest* (video) - boysetsfire
2005: *Dear George* (video) - boysetsfire
2006: *The Misery Index: Notes from the Plague Years* - boysetsfire
2006: *Requiem* (video) - boysetsfire
2007: *Your Last Novelty* - The Casting Out
2007: *The Casting Out* - The Casting Out

2009: *Farewell Show* (DVD) - boysetsfire
2009: *Go Crazy! Throw Fireworks!* - The Casting Out
2010: *The Casting Out!!!* - The Casting Out
2011: *The Ten Count* - The New Recruits
2011: *History Is Written By The Victors* - The New Recruits
2011: Demo - I AM HERESY
2012: *I Am Heresy* - I AM HERESY
2013: *Pigs In Seizure* - I AM HERESY
2013: *Bled Dry* - boysetsfire
2013: *While a Nation Sleeps...* - boysetsfire
2013: *Bled Dry* (video) - boysetsfire
2013: *Closure* (video) - boysetsfire
2013: *Never Said* (video) - boysetsfire
2013: *O Day Star, Son Of Dawn* - I AM HERESY
2014: *Thy Will* - I AM HERESY
2014: *March Of Black Earth* (video) - I AM HERESY
2014: Split 7" (Boysetsfire/Funeral For A Friend)
2015: *NTHN GRY* - Nathan Gray
2015: *Boysetsfire* - boysetsfire
2015: *One Match* (video) - boysetsfire
2017: *Until The Darkness Takes Us* - Nathan Gray Collective

III UNTIL THE DARKNESS TAKES US

Made in the USA
Middletown, DE
31 December 2016